From Joshua to Jesus

*A Brief Chronicle of the Kings, Empires,
Legends and Ideas, that Paved
the Way to Bethlehem*

Andrew Cort

For Marjorie Rose

TABLE OF CONTENTS

Preface

Joshua* and the Israelites entered Canaan around the year 1200 BCE, the same time that the ancient Greeks were besieging Troy as recounted in Homer's *Iliad*. They settled the land by dividing it along family and tribal lines. After Joshua's death, there was no formal centralized system of governance. Israel was a loose confederation, with Elders dispensing justice as needed within their individual Tribes.

The people had never quite finished the task which Moses, on behalf of the Lord, had set before them: other nations and peoples still lived amongst them in the Promised Land. This meant that continuing crises and wars were inevitable, and whenever hostilities broke out one leader or another would arise to meet the challenge. These *ad hoc* chieftains were known as Judges. Some were military leaders such as Gideon, some were solitary heroes such as Samson, some were prophets such as Deborah, some were priests such as Eli.

The system lasted for about a hundred and fifty years, and the main lesson of the whole experience was its inefficiency (not unlike the American *Articles of Confederation*).

Finally, around 1050 BCE, the Judge, Prophet, and High Priest Samuel acquiesced to a growing popular demand for a powerful permanent leader who could put an end to the ceaseless threats from the neighboring Philistines (from whom comes the name 'Palestine'). After a casting of lots he anointed Saul, a strong military man from the tribe of Benjamin, as the first king of Israel.

---

* Joshua's Hebrew name, Je'Hoshea, which means 'God is the Savior', is the same name that is translated in the New Testament as 'Jesus'.

Saul unified the fragmented nation, but his reign would be brief. A bit of a loose cannon, Saul won his first battle with the Philistines, but not without stirring up various conflicts with Samuel, with his own son Jonathan, and with many others.

After the battle with the Philistines was over, Samuel instructed Saul to annihilate the Amalekites, in accordance with the ancient command that is found in *Deuteronomy*: "you shall blot out the memory of Amalek from under heaven. Do not forget!" (*Deut.25.19*) So Saul went to war again and defeated the Amalekites, but he left alive the Amalekite king and all the best livestock. When Samuel found out what Saul had done, he became furious and declared that God regretted making Saul king, since Saul was disobedient. When Samuel turned away, a repentant Saul grabbed him by the clothes and accidentally ripped off a piece, which Samuel then said was a prophecy about what was going to happen to Saul's kingdom: it would be torn from him and given to another. Samuel then commanded that the Amalekite king be brought forth, and Samuel killed him himself. Then he left Saul, never to return.

Samuel grieved over what had transpired, but God told him to cease his grieving and go to the house of Jesse of the tribe of Judah, and there Samuel would find a boy whom the Lord had chosen to be the next king. When Samuel arrived in Bethlehem, Jesse's youngest son David was out tending the flocks. When David returned to his father's house the Lord said to Samuel, "Rise and anoint him, for this is the one." (*1 Sam.16.12*)

CHAPTER ONE

David

David had long been a shepherd of his father's flocks, which means symbolically that, like Moses who for many years was a shepherd to Jethro's flocks, David had been *preparing* himself for his destiny as a shepherd of God's people.

When he returned home that day, and Samuel anointed him, it did not mean that he immediately became the new king; only that he had been selected by God. And for the moment, this was kept secret from Saul.

Oil is the fuel of fire, and 'anointing the head with oil' is a symbol of Confirmation, which means that the Spirit descends into the Mind so that the 'fire' can burn away our ignorance, strengthen our resolve, and clear our vision.[*] So as soon as David (whose name means *well-beloved*) was anointed, the Bible tells us, "the spirit of the Lord gripped David from that day on." Samuel's task is now completed and he departs: "Samuel then set out for Ramah [which means a state of *bliss*]."

Simultaneously, the following sentence then tells us, "the spirit of the Lord had departed from Saul." So Saul, who had earlier been anointed by Samuel, is no longer confirmed as king, the sacrament is reversed, and his vision is no longer clear. In fact, unlike the spirit of the Lord which has just gripped David, "an *evil* spirit from the Lord began to terrify him [italics mine]."

In response to the misery which this 'evil spirit' was causing their king, his courtiers suggested that he find a musician who could soothe him with sweet music

---

[*] The Hebrew word for 'anointing' is *moshach*, from which comes the word *Moshiach*, which means *Messiah*.

whenever the black mood struck. Saul agreed, and when one of them suggested that a certain son of Jesse the Bethlehemite was an excellent lyre player, Saul sent for the boy. So David came walking right into the palace of the oblivious Saul and entered his service. "Whenever the evil spirit of God came upon Saul, David would take the lyre and play it; Saul would find relief and feel better, and the evil spirit would leave him." Of course David, the great psalmist, was no ordinary musician. Saul "took a strong liking to him" and even made him one of the king's arms-bearers.

Meanwhile, the Philistines had regrouped and had once again "assembled their forces for battle." So Saul and his soldiers "drew up their line of battle against the Philistines, with the Philistines stationed on one hill and Israel stationed on the opposite hill."

A champion of the Philistine forces stepped forward; his name was Goliath of Gath, and he was six cubits and a span tall.*(1 Sam.17.4)

Goliath roared at the astonished Israelites, "Why should you come out to engage in battle?"

Choose one of your men and let him come down against me. If he bests me in combat and kills me, we will become your slaves; but if I best him and kill him, you shall be our slaves and serve us.(1 Sam.17.8-9)

Saul and his soldiers, however, were terror-stricken when they beheld this giant. For forty days, Goliath would

---

* More than nine feet.

come forward morning and night and repeat his challenge, but no one took him up on it.

David's three older brothers were serving in Saul's army. David himself was still too young to be a soldier, but one day his father Jesse asked him to bring some food to his brothers who had long been stationed on the hill, and find out how they were doing.

David found his brothers, and while he was speaking to them Goliath came forward and again issued his challenge. David was outraged by this "uncircumcised Philistine" who "dares defy the ranks of the living God." He was also outraged that no soldier had enough trust and certainty in God to accept the giant's challenge. The situation was not unlike the spies' lack of faith when they first reconnoitered Canaan where they also saw giants. So David found Saul and said, "Your servant will go and fight that Philistine."

Saul objected that David was "only a boy." But David knew he was fully prepared and had nothing to fear.

> *Your servant has been tending his father's*
> *sheep, and if a lion or a bear came and*
> *carried off an animal from the flock, I would*
> *go after it and fight it and rescue it from its*
> *mouth. And if it attacked me, I would seize it*
> *by the beard and strike it down and kill it.*
> *Your servant has killed both lion and bear;*
> *and that uncircumcised Philistine shall end*
> *up like one of them, for he has defied the*
> *ranks of the living God. (1 Sam.17.32-36)*

In other words, David makes clear, it is not his *own* power that will overcome Goliath. It is his perfect faith in God that will ensure his success. "The Lord," David went on, "who saved me from the lion and the bear will also save me from that Philistine." So Saul eventually assented, sent him off, and said, "may the Lord be with you!" Then David, who refused any armor or a sword, put a few stones in his shepherd's bag, took his slingshot, and "went toward the Philistine."

Goliath, of course, laughed when he saw him, telling the boy to come closer so he could feed his flesh to the birds and beasts. But David just said, "This very day the Lord will deliver you into my hands."

We all know the story, a story which has inspired countless feats of glory against insurmountable odds. "David put his hand into his bag; he took out a stone and slung it. It struck the Philistine in the forehead; the stone sank into his forehead, and he fell face down on the ground." David then ran up and stood over the giant. Since he had no sword of his own, he took Goliath's sword and cut off his head.

"When the Philistines saw that their warrior was dead, they ran." Fittingly, their hero had been destroyed by *stone* – the very symbol of the low level of material Being which the Philistines represent – which now sank into his own forehead and destroyed his *mind*. "The men of Israel and Judah[*] rose up with a war cry and pursued the Philistines.... [Many] fell mortally wounded along the road.... Then the Israelites returned from chasing the Philistines and looted their camp."

David, of course, was thereafter revered by the people as a great hero. Even Saul's own son Jonathan, the heir to the throne, "loved David as himself". He now symbolically turned over his royal birthright to David: "Jonathan took off the cloak and tunic he was wearing and gave them to David, together with his sword, bow, and belt." This transference of power, and the clear recognition that David

---

[*] Here is an early mention of the internal tensions that will eventually lead to the later historical division of the Israelite tribes into two separate kingdoms, 'Israel' and 'Judah'.

is God's true 'elect', is also symbolized as Saul gives his daughter, the princess Michal, in marriage to David. It is further recognized when David and the soldiers return from their pursuit of the defeated Philistines, and "the women of all the towns of Israel came out singing and dancing" and even sang the song, "Saul has slain his thousands; David, his tens of thousands!"

Needless to say, all of this made King Saul insanely jealous. He tried on several occasions to kill David, but "the Lord was with him" and David always escaped. So he tried sending him off at the head of soldiers to fight in the endless wars with the Philistines, hoping that David would meet his end at their hands. But "David was successful in all his undertakings", and as a result, everyone just loved him all the more. Saul then conspired to have messengers kill David in his sleep, but Michal heard of the plot, warned her husband, and helped him escape. When Saul's messengers came in the morning, David was gone and all they found was an idol which Michal had placed in his bed as a decoy. Confronted by her father for helping his enemy escape, Michal lied and said that David had said "Help me get away or I'll kill you."

David fled to Ramah (which, according to the books of Samuel and Jeremiah, was the burial place of Rachel), and joined Samuel. Saul heard that he was there, and three times he sent messengers to seize him. But 'Ramah', *bliss*, is a high state of Being. The 'Above' cannot be stormed by the 'Below'. Each time Saul's messengers came to Ramah, they "saw a band of prophets speaking in ecstasy, with Samuel standing by as their leader, and the spirit of God came upon Saul's messengers and they too began to speak in ecstasy." Finally, Saul came himself, but "the spirit of God came upon him too; and he walked on speaking in ecstasy, until he reached Naioth in Ramah." There, he "stripped off his clothes" before Samuel.

Samuel and his 'band of prophets' would have been a spiritual school, and David had come to be initiated. They spoke "in ecstasy" in Ramah, for Samuel and his enlightened initiates experienced the joy and exaltation of the direct experience of divine reality.

Saul had been initiated by Samuel previously, when he was first named king. "The Lord herewith anoints you ruler over His own people", Samuel had said, and he then gave Saul a series of ceremonial instructions that are filled with esoteric symbolism. These involved a trip to Rachel's tomb; a message from his own father; a visit from three men on a pilgrimage to God who would come to him bearing bread, wine, and three lambs; and a journey Saul was to take to the 'Hill of God'. There, Samuel had told him, "you will encounter a band of prophets coming down from the shrine, preceded by lyres, timbrels, flutes and harps, and they will be speaking in ecstasy. The spirit of the Lord will grip you, and you will speak in ecstasy along with them; you will become another man." Saul did everything Samuel told him to do. So Saul was initiated and was *reborn* as a new man. But later on he disobeyed God's command to completely annihilate *doubt* (that is, he failed to completely annihilate the Amalekites: the word 'Amalek' means *doubt*). He therefore 'fell', and now when he returns to Ramah in his endeavor to kill David he "stripped off his clothes": the return to nakedness is a symbol of his return to ignorance and subservience, "and he lay naked all that day and all night."

David then left Ramah, and Saul continued his pursuit, chasing him all over the country. But David always eluded him, and Saul knew his days were numbered.

During this period, David and his men fought their own battle against the Amalekites. The Amalekites, in typical fashion, had raided David's camp when he and his soldiers were away, and had taken women and children captive as well as their goods and possessions. David, whose troops were exhausted and embittered upon returning to the empty camp, inquired of the Lord whether he should go in pursuit immediately. God responded, "Pursue, for you shall overtake and you shall rescue." So David went to battle with four hundred soldiers, and they soon came upon the Amalekite camp and found them "eating and drinking and making merry because of all the vast spoil they had taken from the land of the Philistines and from the land of Judah." David attacked, and permitted none to live, although four hundred of them managed to mount camels and escape (no matter how hard we try to have faith, some doubt always survives). All the women and children, and all the stolen possessions, were rescued.

Samuel then passed away, and shortly after his death Saul had to lead his army one last time into battle with the Philistines. Before this battle, unlike David who had inquired of *God*, Saul actually sought the services of a *witch* whom he ordered to conjure up the spirit of Samuel so that Saul could seek his advice (the Law of Moses had declared such activities *illegal*, but had never said they were *ineffective*!) So the spirit of Samuel came, expressed much displeasure at being disturbed, and told Saul pointblank that he stood no chance at all in this fight with the Philistines, for God was no longer with him.

Nevertheless, Saul was not a coward and he bravely led his forces into battle despite the odds. There he watched three of his sons, including Jonathan, die before his eyes, and was himself severely wounded. Lest he fall into the hands of the enemy, he fell on his sword and died. (Later, the text says that an Amalekite appeared before the mortally wounded king, and at Saul's own request the Amalekite 'finished him off'. Thus was Saul destroyed in the end by the very *doubt* he had allowed to linger).

When David heard the news, he wept for Saul and Jonathan, and he sang a funeral dirge that began,

Your glory, O Israel,
Lies slain on your heights;
How the mighty have fallen! (2 Sam.1.19)

Shortly afterward, David asked the Lord if he should go up to one of the towns of Judah, and God said 'Yes', that he should go to Hebron. So he journeyed to Hebron with his family and his followers. It was 1005 BCE. And the people of Judah came, "and there they anointed David king over the House of Judah."

But Abner, Saul's army commander, had taken Saul's surviving son, Ish-bosheth, and proclaimed him king of Israel.

Thus began the great schism between Judah and Israel, and seven years of civil war followed. During that time, Ish-bosheth was murdered in his sleep (Abner had already been killed), and once again David mourned at the death of his enemy.

Then the nation reunited, and would remain so for a little while:

All the tribes of Israel came to David at
Hebron and said, "We are your own
flesh and blood. Long before now, when
Saul was king over us, it was you who
led Israel out and led Israel in; and the
Lord said to you: You shall shepherd My
people Israel; you shall be ruler of
Israel." All the elders of Israel came to
the king at Hebron, and King David
made a pact with them in Hebron before
the Lord. And they anointed David
king over Israel. (2 Sam.5.1-3)

David was thirty years old when he first became king. He ruled over Judah for seven years. He would now rule over Judah and Israel combined for thirty-three years.

His first act as ruler of the united kingdom was to wisely move his capital city from Hebron, in the North, to Jerusalem – a Jebusite city that sat in between the two parts of the kingdom and had been neutral during the years of fighting. After two hundred years of failing to fulfill God's directive, David and the Israelites finally chased out the Jebusites, and their city of Jerusalem became the City of David.

Mount Moriah, where Abraham bound Isaac, is said to be a hill in Jerusalem. This mountain, which Abraham called 'the Mountain of the Lord', is believed in Jewish mysticism to be the holy center, the Foundation, of the whole world, the place where heaven and earth 'kiss'. It is also believed to be the spot where Jacob dreamt of a ladder ascending to heaven. When he awoke, Jacob said, "How awesome is this place! This is none other than the abode of God." Today, the same spot is marked by an Islamic shrine, the Dome of the Rock. The rock in the center of the dome is believed by Muslims to be the spot from which Muhammad ascended to God accompanied by the angel Gabriel, and was given the obligatory Islamic prayers. For Christians, Jerusalem is the scene of many key events in the life of Jesus, including the Crucifixion and the Resurrection. These are all just a few of the special claims of the universal city of Jerusalem.

After King David made Jerusalem his capital, the first thing he did was to go to war against the Philistines, and he finally succeeded in expelling them from the Promised Land. Next, he purchased Mount Moriah, which sits on the northern boundary of the city. He then assembled a troop of chosen soldiers, and returned to Judah to retrieve the Ark of the Covenant and bring it to Jerusalem.

On their return to Jerusalem, "David and all the House of Israel danced before the Lord to the sound of all kinds of cypress wood instruments, with lyres, harps, timbrels, sistrums, and cymbals" – a scene corresponding to Samuel and his band of prophets speaking in ecstasy.

David whirled with all his might before
the Lord.... Thus David and all the House
of Israel brought up the Ark of the Lord
with shouts and with blasts of the horn.
(2 Sam.6.14-15)

They brought the Ark into a tent that David had specially pitched for it on Mount Moriah, and David sacrificed Burnt Offerings and Peace Offerings. He then blessed the people in the name of the Lord, and distributed bread, meat, and wine, to everyone. Then all the people returned to their homes.

But Saul's daughter Michal, a wife of David (he by now had several), had watched the return of the Ark through her window, and she saw David dancing and whirling in his linen tunic before the Ark. She scorned his behavior as frivolous and unworthy of a king, and when he returned to his household she reprimanded him with sarcasm: "Didn't the king of Israel do himself honor today – exposing himself today in the sight of the slavegirls of his subjects, as one of the riffraff might expose himself!"

David, however, was not impressed by the mere external appearance of so-called 'dignified' behavior, and he told Michal that he *would* dance before the Lord, and he *would* humble himself in his own eyes and in the eyes of the people, and as a result of this, "among the slavegirls that you speak of I will be honored." God reproved Michal for her haughty strait-laced attitude, and "to her dying day Michal daughter of Saul had no children." (This certainly should be useful food for thought for many people who convince themselves that joy and dance and music and celebration are inappropriate and sinful ways of worshipping God.)

David was now settled in his palace, the Ark was home, and the nation was safe. He spoke to the prophet Nathan and said, "Here I am dwelling in a house of cedar, while the Ark of the Lord abides in a tent!" Nathan suggested that David go and do "whatever you have in mind, for the Lord is with you." But later that night, God came to Nathan and told him to go back to David and tell the king that He, the Lord, would build *David* a house (that is, a 'dynasty'), but it would be David's *son*, not David himself, who would in turn build a house (the Temple) for the Lord. "When your days are done and you lie with your fathers, I will raise up your offspring after you, one of your own issue, and I will establish his kingship. He shall build a house for My name, and I will establish his royal throne forever." When David heard this, he did not question God's decision or complain in any way. He thanked the Lord for His promise, and said, "may Your Name be glorified forever."

David still has two negative qualities that must be overcome before God's Temple can be built (which, speaking esoterically, is a symbol for attaining a higher internal level of Being). He still has an angry emotional tendency toward violence and an out-of-control lustfulness.

The story of why David is not permitted to build the Temple begins one afternoon during a war with Ammon, when "David rose from his couch and strolled on the roof of the royal palace; and from the roof he saw a woman bathing. The woman was very beautiful, and the king sent someone to make inquiries about the woman. He reported, 'She is Bathsheba daughter of Eliam, and wife of Uriah the Hittite.'" Uriah was one of David's generals, and he was away serving with Joab, David's right-hand-man, in the war against Ammon.

> *David sent messengers to fetch her; she*
> *came to him and he lay with her ... and she*
> *went back home. The woman conceived, and*
> *she sent word to David, "I am pregnant."*
> *Thereupon David sent a message to Joab,*
> *"Send Uriah the Hittite to me"; and Joab*
> *sent Uriah to David. (2.Sam.11.4-6)*

When the puzzled Uriah appeared, David asked him how things were going in the war. Then David told him to go and relax at his house before returning to the fight. But Uriah, feeling guilty about the men he had left behind in battle, would not go home: he slept outside. When David found this out, he told Uriah to remain in Jerusalem a second night before returning to the front. That night, David entertained him and got him good and drunk: but *still* Uriah would not go home and sleep with his wife. Now this was a big problem, for David needed Uriah to spend a night with Bathsheba, so that when the child was born it would appear to be the legitimate child of her husband. Since this was plainly not working, David became angry and he took desperate measures. He sent the following note to Joab: "Place Uriah in the front line where the fighting is fiercest; then fall back so that he may be killed."

Everything went according to plan.

> *When Uriah's wife heard that her husband*
> *Uriah was dead, she lamented over her*
> *husband. After the period of mourning was over,*
> *David sent and had her brought to the palace;*
> *she became his wife and she bore him a son.*
> *(2 Sam.11.26-27)*

God, however, was not at all pleased by this turn of events, and He sent Nathan once again to speak with David.

Nathan came and informed the king that there was a rich man in the kingdom with many flocks and herds, and a poor man who only had one small lamb, which he took great care of and treated like his own child. Recently, the rich man had had a visitor. But he was loath to kill one of his lambs to prepare a dinner, so he stole and slaughtered the poor man's lamb instead. David flew into a rage when he heard this. "As the Lord lives", he said, "the man who did this deserves to die! He shall pay for the lamb four times over, because he did such a thing and showed no pity." And Nathan said to David, "That man is you!"

For what he has done to Uriah, Nathan says, God has declared that "the sword shall never depart from your house.... I will make a calamity rise against you from within your own house; I will take your wives and give them to another man before your very eyes and he shall sleep with your wives under this very sun."

> *"You acted in secret, but I will make this*
> *happen in the sight of all Israel and in broad*
> *daylight." David said to Nathan,*
> *"I stand guilty before the Lord!"*
> *(2 Sam.12.12-13)*

Nathan tells David that in view of this repentance the Lord has decided to let him live. The child, however, would not survive.

This is in *internal symbol*. The 'result' of David's violence, greedy lustfulness, and the wrong mixing of influences, cannot survive. David understands this, but he also now learns to show mercy and kindness – qualities that were missing in his treatment of Uriah. When the child became critically ill, David entreated the lord on the child's behalf, and he fasted and prayed and slept on the floor in the child's room. And when the child died on the seventh day, David consoled his wife Bathsheba. The Lord then forgave David, Bathsheba conceived again, and she bore another son whom she named Solomon. Solomon was thus the child of love, mercy and kindness.

Even so, there are always consequences, obligatory responses, to our external and internal actions. The 'punishment' that God said would occur is exactly what had to happen. Later in the story, another of David's sons, Absalom, would take up the sword against his father, David would have to flee from Jerusalem, there would be a calamitous war, and Absalom would fulfill God's prediction by sleeping "with his father's concubines with the full knowledge of all Israel." In the end, David would prevail, and then once again he would mourn the death of an enemy. "O my son, my son Absalom! If only I had died instead of you! O Absalom, my son, my son!"

The Bible does not condone David's cruel and sinful behavior. But he is always portrayed as a fallible and vulnerable human being, and it is his humility, his genuine repentance, his acceptance of responsibility, his love and forgiveness toward his enemies, and his unfaltering love of God, that shine throughout the story and differentiate him from the rest of us.

David's confession is preserved in Psalm 51: "A psalm of David, when Nathan the prophet came to him after he had come to Bathsheba:"

Have mercy upon me, O God,
as befits Your faithfulness;
in keeping with Your abundant compassion,
blot out my transgressions.
Wash me thoroughly of my iniquity,
and purify me of my sin;

for I recognize my transgressions,
and am ever conscious of my sin.

...

Lord, open my lips,
and let my mouth declare Your praise.
You do not want me to bring sacrifices;
You do not desire burnt offerings;
True sacrifice to God is a contrite spirit.

The Death of King David

Many ancient peoples believed that the safety of the people, and even the prosperity and fertility of the entire world, were bound up with the life, strength, and potency of their king. When a king grew old and feeble, it was oftentimes customary to slaughter the king, so that his soul, before becoming completely ineffective and sterile, could move on to a successor. The Israelites did not follow this barbaric custom, but the symbolic significance of the declining potency of their king did not escape them.

Absalom had fulfilled God's prophecy and defied his father by having sexual relations with David's concubines. This is a standard act of usurpation of a king's power by the king's son. The Titan, Cronus, usurped his father Uranus by castrating him, so that Uranus could no longer seed the world through the goddess Gaia. The same symbol of castration occurs in the legend of Noah and Ham. Jacob's time drew toward an end when his son Reuben entered Jacob's tent and lay with his father's concubine. Now Absalom has done the same thing to David.

Jacob did not immediately die, and neither does David. Reuben did not become the heir, and neither does Absalom. But the potency of the king is at an end, and the transference of power is imminent. Jacob had no further children after the act of usurpation by his son, and neither does David. After the defeat of Absalom,

> *David went to his palace in Jerusalem, and*
> *the king took the ten concubines he had left*
> *to mind the palace and put them in a*
> *guarded place; he provided for them, but he*
> *did not cohabit with them. They remained in*
> *seclusion until the day they died,*
> *in living widowhood. (2 Sam.20.3)*

Shortly thereafter, we are told, the last of his strength, his inner 'heat', began to dissipate. "King David was now old, advanced in years; and though they covered him with bedclothes, he never felt warm." His courtiers made a final attempt to revive their king's potency:

> *His courtiers said to him, "let a young*
> *virgin be sought for my lord the king, to*
> *wait upon Your Majesty and be his*
> *attendant, and let her lie in your bosom,*
> *and my lord the king will be warm." So*
> *they looked for a beautiful girl throughout*
> *the territory of Israel. They found Abishag*
> *the Shunammite and brought her to the*
> *king. The girl was exceedingly beautiful.*
> *She became the king's attendant*
> *and waited upon him; but the king was not*
> *intimate with her. (1 Kings.1.1-4)*

Once it was clear that his inner force was gone, another son of David, Adonijah, son of Haggith, stepped forward presumptuously to claim his father's throne. But Adonijah was not meant to be a king. He was spoiled and superficial, and he did not have the wisdom to be a king.

His father had never scolded him: "Why
did you do that?" He was the one born
after Absalom, and, like him,
was very handsome. (1 Kings.1.6)

Nonetheless, he garnered the support of David's military commander, Joab, plus the priest, Abiathar, as well as several of his younger brothers, and all the king's courtiers of the tribe of Judah. He held a sacrificial feast inviting all these supporters, and he assumed the kingship. But he did not invite Nathan the Prophet, Zadok the Priest, or his brother Solomon.

Nathan sought out Bathsheba, and they each went to the king and reminded him that he had sworn an oath by the Lord that Solomon would succeed him as king. David said he would fulfill his oath immediately.

"Take my loyal soldiers, and have my son
Solomon ride on my mule and bring him
down to Gihon [the 'valley of Grace'].
Let the priest Zadok and the prophet
Nathan anoint him there king over Israel,
whereupon you shall sound the horn and
shout 'Long live King Solomon!'
Then march up after him, and let him come
in and sit on my throne.
For he shall succeed me as king;
him I designate to be the ruler of
Israel and Judah."(1 Kings.1.32-35)

After the ceremony, as Solomon reentered Jerusalem on David's noble mule, scores of people marched behind him, dancing, playing music, and shouting "Long live King

Solomon!" Adonijah and his companions were still at their feast, and they heard the uproar. A messenger came and told them what all the noise was about. "Thereupon, all of Adonijah's guests rose in alarm and each went his own way." Adonijah himself, in great fear, ran to the Tabernacle and "grasped the horns of the altar" – a way of claiming sanctuary. When King Solomon was informed of this, he said, "If he behaves worthily, not a hair of his head shall fall to the ground; but if he is caught in any offense, he shall die." Solomon then sent for him, Adonijah came to the palace and bowed before him, and Solomon told him to "Go home".

Now, just before David's life draws to a close, he gives the new king some final advice – advice which is still traditionally given to a young Jewish boy as part of the Bar Mitzvah ritual when he turns thirteen:

> *"I am going the way of all the earth;*
> *be strong and show yourself a man.*
> *Keep the charge of the Lord your God,*
> *walking in His ways and following His laws,*
> *His commandments, His rules,*
> *and His admonitions as recorded in the*
> *Teaching of Moses, in order that you may*
> *succeed in whatever you undertake*
> *and wherever you turn." (1 Kings.2.2-3)*

Further, David advises, there are several rebellious and antagonistic subjects whom Solomon will now have to bring into line or destroy.

Joab, for instance, who had long been David's friend and right-hand-man, had betrayed David in the end, and had turned against the proper ruler: Joab had unnecessarily caused the death (rather than the capture) of Absalom, and then rebuked the king for mourning his own son; he had killed David's nephew, Amasa, when David tried to replace Joab with Amasa; and he had supported Adonijah in the boy's attempt to usurp the throne. "So act in accordance with your wisdom," David says to Solomon, "and see that his white hair does not go down to Sheol in peace."

Solomon will also have to deal with Shimei, a member of Saul's family who had insulted David and thrown stones at him when the king fled Jerusalem during the rebellion of Absalom. Later, when Shimei groveled and apologized, David had sworn not to put him to the sword. Now, however, David advises Solomon, "do not let him go unpunished; for you are a wise man and you will know how to deal with him and send his gray hair down to Sheol in blood."

This is not a biblical sanction of literal vengefulness and murder. It is a symbolic inner admonition to cleanse the soul before 'building the Temple'. David knows that Wisdom at the level of Solomon cannot be tainted by the arrogant contempt represented by Shimei or the treachery and faithlessness represented by Joab. These qualities must be immediately placed 'Below' in 'Sheol'.

> *So David slept with his fathers, and he was*
> *buried in the City of David.... And Solomon*
> *sat upon the throne of his father David, and*
> *his rule was firmly established.*
> *(1 Kings.2.10-12)*

CHAPTER TWO

Solomon

As soon as David was gone, Adonijah tried again. He did not challenge Solomon directly, but he cleverly went to Solomon's mother, Bathsheba, and asked her to intervene on his behalf and get the king to give him Abishag as his wife. After all, he told Bathsheba, "he won't refuse you."

The request was hardly innocent: Adonijah was trying yet again to usurp David's throne, this time by sleeping with his concubine, as his brother Absalom had done. Of course, the whole attempt was a preposterous caricature. The throne had already passed, Abishag had never had sexual relations with David, and Adonijah did not even have the courage to speak to his brother Solomon face to face. Solomon immediately recognized the threat, the cowardice, and the ineffectualness. All of this had to be eliminated (not just from the kingdom, but symbolically from the ascending soul), so Solomon instructed his new right-hand-man, Benaiah, to strike down and kill Adonijah.

Solomon then continued to sweep clean and purify the soul. First, he dismissed Abiathar, a priest who had supported Adonijah's original attempt to take the throne from David, and he banished him. He did not have him executed, however, because Abiathar had "carried the Ark of my Lord God before my father David and because you shared all the hardships that my father endured."

When Joab, who had also supported Adonijah, heard of all that had happened, he fled to the Tabernacle for sanctuary. Solomon sent Benaiah to bring him out and kill him, but Joab refused to come out, saying, "I will die here." So Solomon instructed Benaiah to do "just as he said":

Benaiah returned to the Tabernacle and struck Joab down right there. (He had given up his claim to sanctuary by *choosing* to die there.)

As for Shimei, Solomon told him that he would be spared, but he was to build himself a home in Jerusalem and never leave the city. "This is fair," Shimei said, "your servant will do just as my lord the king has spoken". But three years later, Shimei left the city to pursue two runaway slaves. When he returned, Solomon gave Benaiah orders to strike him down as well.

This was the remnant of negativity and corruption that had turned against God's Will and had to be cleansed by Solomon. Abiathar even *means* 'father of the remnant'. Adonijah means 'the Lord is my master', but the place in the psyche represented by Adonijah had turned away and betrayed the Lord, and repeatedly *defied* the master. Joab, David's great military general, represented David's *Will*, and his name means 'voluntary'. But he, too, had turned away from his master and become dangerous and defiant. Shimei means 'that which hears and obeys', but once again, this place in the psyche had turned away, listened only to its *own* voice, and had refused to obey what was higher. Solomon eliminated all of this, and thus, the text concludes, "the kingdom was secured in Solomon's hands."

All these psychological aspects felt that *they knew better*. They represent the beliefs and opinions that we cherish but rarely examine, the ones that are poorly reasoned, often contradictory, and usually indefensible and absurd. Solomon has swept them clean so that he can rise beyond them and achieve genuine Wisdom.

Now, to increase his power through alliances, we are immediately told that "Solomon allied himself by marriage with Pharaoh king of Egypt. He married Pharaoh's daughter and brought her to the City of David...."

Solomon then traveled to Gibeon (which means 'lifted up'), and there he had a dream. In his dream, the Lord appeared to Solomon and told him to ask for whatever he wanted and it would be granted. Solomon thanked Him, and then said, "Grant, then, Your servant an understanding mind to judge Your people, to distinguish between good and bad."

The Lord was pleased that Solomon had
asked for this. And God said to him,
"Because you asked for this – you did not
ask for long life, you did not ask for riches,
you did not ask for the life of your enemies,
but you asked for discernment in dispensing
justice – I now do as you have spoken. I
grant you a wise and discerning mind; there
has never been anyone like you before, nor
will anyone like you arise again. And I also
grant you what you did not ask for – both
riches and glory all your life – the like of
which no king has ever had."
(1 Kings.3.10-13)

This granting of wisdom such as "has never been", represents the opening of what Plato will call *Nous,* the Eye of the Soul. It indicates a state of Enlightenment above our ordinary day-to-day consciousness. The lesson here is that an awakened *Nous* must be earned, it must be asked for, and it must be desired above all other things. It then comes, if it comes, as a gift from Above.

The dream is followed by the famous story of the two women who came to Solomon with a baby, each claiming to be the child's mother, and asking Solomon to decide between them. Solomon listened to their accounts, and then ordered that a sword be brought and the child cut in half, so that they could share the baby equally. One of the women, however, pleaded with the king, "Please, my lord, give her the live child; only don't kill it!" Solomon could 'see' at once, of course, that this was the child's real mother, and returned the baby to her.

In the inner story, the soul now recognizes the true authority (*Nous*), and subordinates itself to Solomon's will:

> *When all Israel heard the decision that the*
> *king had rendered, they stood in awe of the*
> *king; for they saw that he possessed divine*
> *wisdom to execute justice.*
> *King Solomon was now king over all Israel.*
> *(1 Kings.3.29 – 4.1)*

It was time to build the Temple.

Solomon's Temple, the permanent 'home for God' where the Ark of the Covenant would rest and the *Shechinah*** would dwell, was of course built on the same pattern and initiatory sequence as the original 'Tabernacle in the Wilderness' that was built by Moses, though it was far more grand and elaborate.

The Bible tells us that "no hammer or ax or any iron tool was heard in the House while it was being built." The Talmud comments on this verse by suggesting that because the Temple was constructed to enrich human life, and iron implements are so often used to destroy human life, it would not have been fitting to use iron tools when building the Temple.

But some tales suggest that there was even more to the story. The Scriptures say that in addition to his unsurpassed wisdom regarding 'good' and 'evil' and 'justice', and his thousands of songs and proverbs, Solomon "discoursed

---

* The *Shechinah*, in Jewish tradition, is God's 'Presence' in the material Creation, the 'Bride of God', the Feminine aspect of Divinity.

about trees, from the cedar in Lebanon to the hyssop that grows out of the wall; and he discoursed about beasts, birds, creeping things, and fishes." Legends, however, claim that Solomon did not merely discourse *about* these plants and animals: *he spoke with them.* God had granted him so much wisdom, that Solomon understood the language of every living thing. And not just plants and animals. Solomon could converse with angels and demons. He could even drive demons out, when they possessed human beings.

One of the greatest challenges to Solomon's wisdom was to find a way to build the Lord's Temple without using iron tools to cut, fashion, smooth down, and fit the great stones together. Solomon knew that God never gives us more obstacles to overcome than we are capable of handling, so the injunction in the Torah against the use of iron tools had to mean that another method existed. So he called together all the wise of his kingdom, and asked if any of them knew the secret.

An old wizard, learned in ancient lore, revealed to Solomon that on the sixth day of Creation, in addition to many other Wonders, God had created the Shamir. This little stone (some say it was a little worm), the size of a grain of barley, was used by Moses to engrave the names of the Tribes onto the twelve precious stones in the ephod worn by the High Priest. The Shamir, the wizard knew, could slice stone, and would be able to cut the stones for the Temple in complete silence.

But neither he, nor any other of the assembled wise, knew where the Shamir might be.

So Solomon called together all the demons who were under his control, but they also had no idea where the Shamir was located. They suspected, however, that their leader, Asmodeus, the king of the demons, probably knew the secret.

They told Solomon the name of a mountain where Asmodeus dwelt. Further, they informed him that there was a spring of pure water within this mountain from which Asmodeus drank. Each day he would drink his fill, and then seal the well with a great rock before going about his business. When he returned, he would always check the rock to be sure the seal had not been tampered with during his absence, and when he was satisfied he would remove the rock and drink again. [The demon's 'water', which signifies the level of 'truth' with which he sustains himself and his power, comes from the spring 'Below'. Each day, before drinking, he would make sure that nothing had entered it from 'Above'].

Solomon called for his General and right-hand-man, Benaiah (whose name means 'son of the Lord'), and they devised a plan to capture Asmodeus. Benaiah went forth to the demon's mountain, with a chain, a bundle of wool, a container of wine, and Solomon's signet ring upon which the old wizard had inscribed the Name of God.

When Benaiah arrived at the mountain he bored a hole at the bottom, letting out all the water without touching the great stone on top. Then he stopped up the hole with some of his wool. Next, he went to the other side of the mountain, to a spot higher up, and bored another hole. Through this hole he refilled the great well with wine, and then stopped up the hole with the rest of his wool.

When Asmodeus returned, he was astonished to find wine instead of water in his well, for the seal had not been touched. At first, he would not drink of it, but soon he succumbed to his thirst and drank deeply until his senses were overpowered and the wine put him into a deep sleep.

Benaiah now came forth from his hiding place, slipped the ring with the Name of God onto the chain, and put the chain around the neck of the king of demons.

Asmodeus awoke and tried to escape, but the chain with the Name could not be resisted, and Benaiah led him off and returned to Solomon.

Solomon spoke with Asmodeus and demanded that he reveal the hiding place of the Shamir. The demon said that God had given the Shamir to the Angel of the Sea, and the Angel had long ago entrusted it to a great bird, who had taken an oath to guard it carefully. The job of this bird is to seek out mountains that are too rocky to be inhabited, to use the Shamir to break up the rock, and then to fill the openings with seeds so that plants begin to grow and the mountains soon become habitable. But there are many, many, such places amongst the southern mountains where the bird might be, and Asmodeus could help no further.

Once again, Solomon and Benaiah devised a plan. Benaiah took an expeditionary force in search of the great bird. Eventually they found its nest, and as Solomon had expected it was full of fledglings. Following Solomon's plan, Benaiah covered the nest with a flat transparent stone he had brought with him. Then he hid himself and waited.

When the great bird returned and saw her hungry, helpless, fledglings beneath the stone, she took out the Shamir to break the stone. Benaiah then jumped out from his hiding place, yelling and waving his arms, and the terrified bird dropped the Shamir and flew off.

Benaiah picked up the Shamir, removed the stone from the nest, and returned to King Solomon.

The tiny Shamir, representing just a tiny fraction of the force of God, is so strong that it can "cut stone" – that is, it can cut through the denseness and hardness of the material world. This enormous power can only be located (it is somewhere *within oneself*) with the help of our dark side, the 'evil inclination', which must be tamed. The demonic King Asmodeus is the dark negative analogue of King Solomon. (In a later legend, Asmodeus even replaces Solomon for a time as king, and no one notices.)

On one level (the bird soaring through the mountains), the Shamir breaks through 'stone' to make habitations for human beings. But when employed by the wisdom of Solomon, it breaks through *our* 'stone' to make a habitation (a Temple) for God.

Once Solomon knew that the stones could be cut and fitted without the noise or violence of iron tools, the task of construction began. For this, the Bible tells us that Solomon called upon the services of two special friends, both of whom were named Hiram. The story of this triad of Temple Builders would later provide a basis for the Freemason tradition.

First, there was King Hiram of Tyre, who "had always been a friend of David." Solomon knew that no one among the Israelites knew how to cut timber the way Hiram's people did, so he made a contract with Hiram whereby Hiram would supply cedar trees from Lebanon for the Temple and Solomon would provide food and supplies for the workers. In addition to the wood, Solomon "ordered huge blocks of choice stone to be quarried, so that the foundations of the house might be laid with hewn stones. Solomon's masons, Hiram's masons, and the men of Gebal [a name which refers to cutting *'boundaries' or 'limits'*] shaped them. Thus the timber and the stones for the building were made ready."

To make the furnishings that would be placed *within* Temple, Solomon sent for the other Hiram. "He was the son of a widow of the tribe of Naphtali, and his father had been a Tyrian, a coppersmith." Solomon himself would make all the furnishings that were to be placed within the inner sanctuary and the Holy of Holies, but Hiram made everything else. "He was endowed with skill, ability, and talent for executing all work in bronze."

This Hiram, the master craftsman, represents the *active* force of this triad. King Hiram, who supplies the materials – the cedar wood and stone – represents the *material* force. The name 'Hiram' means both *destroyer* and *exaltation*, so one Hiram would chop down trees and cut materials into pieces, while the other would take this raw material and build them up into magnificent new constructions – such as columns, lavers, bowls, decorative pomegranates, and statuettes of lions, oxen, and cherubim.

All of this was overseen by the wisdom of Solomon, the *reconciling* force of the triad of Builders.

Hiram made his objects out of copper and bronze, but everything Solomon made he made out of gold. For example:

> *And Solomon made all the furnishings that*
> *were in the House of the Lord: the altar, of*
> *gold; the table for the bread of display, of*
> *gold; the lampstands – five on the right side,*
> *and five on the left ... of gold.*
> *(1 Kings.7.48-50)*

Where did all this gold come from? Partly, no doubt, from trade and tariffs – Israel was a necessary trade route for many caravans. But stories and legends abound about 'Solomon the Magician' and 'Solomon the Alchemist', who knew the secret of turning base metal into gold and who could therefore supply God's Temple with all the gold imaginable. In their inner symbolic meaning, these mythological stories are perfectly true. The alchemical transmutation of base matter into 'gold' is an allegory for an Initiate's inner transmutation of base levels of Being into sacred levels of Being – that is, *spiritual* 'gold' – and the story means this inner work was accomplished by Solomon.

When this symbolism is understood, it is really rather humorous to picture modern chemists in their laboratories trying literally to follow the symbolic instructions written down by medieval alchemists, failing to produce any gold in their test tubes, and then solemnly declaring that alchemy does not work and they have 'proven' it!

It is also easy to see how these stories of Temple craftsmen, overseen by the high triad of Wisdom, Cosmic Resources, and Demiurgic Action, could lead to the metaphorical association of masonry with inner spiritual work, and a close relationship of craftsmen with the priesthood. Like alchemy, the 'building of the Temple' represents an *inner spiritual achievement.* The literal building of a structure of wood and stone is its symbol.

Hiram the craftsman, (who is sometimes called CHiram Abiff), has a special place of honor in the lore of Freemasonry. The Bible does not tell us about the death of CHiram, but according to the traditions of Freemasonry he was foully murdered. It seems that CHiram divided his workforce into three groups, according to their level of mastery. Each group had special passwords and other signs by which their level of excellence and skill could be immediately recognized and appreciated. Some, of course, were dissatisfied, believing themselves worthy of a more exalted position. One night, three such malcontents lay in wait, attacked CHiram, and when he still refused to reveal the 'Master's Word' (which only he, the Master, knew) they killed him with their tools. They buried his body on Mount Moriah (that is, at the gateway between matter and spirit) and fled. But they were soon captured and executed by King Solomon. To the Freemasons, CHiram is a martyr, and the 'Master's Word' (that is, the secret of the Temple, his secret Teaching) has been lost to us until his resurrection.

Again, as *myth*, this undoubtedly-fabricated story is *true*. Lower forces of the soul are always prone to jealousy and indignation, believing they are worthy of more respect, and each one of us has an inner 'mob' that is always prepared to depose or even murder the true ruler of the soul. Actually, this is a snapshot of the usual state of our inner lives. The terrifying risk here is that real Truth and real Hope might then be lost for a very long time or even forever, unless it is preserved and protected by a 'secret society' (inner or outer), pending a safer and more favorable moment in time.

Solomon's Temple was at last completed and Solomon "convoked all the elders of Israel – all the heads of the tribes and the ancestral chieftains of the Israelites", so that the Temple could be formally dedicated. The priests carried the Ark of the Covenant, containing the Tablets with the Ten Commandments, into the Holy of Holies: (the wings of the Cherubim – the 'Mercy Seat' – spread over the Ark and protected it from view.) When they set the Ark down, the *Shechinah* appeared, and they had to leave the shrine: "[T]he priests were not able to remain and perform the service because of the cloud, for the Presence of the Lord filled the House of the Lord." (The same thing had happened when the Tabernacle was completed.) Then Solomon said:

> *The Lord has chosen*
> *To abide in a thick cloud:*
> *I have now built for You*
> *A stately House.*
> *A place where You*
> *May dwell forever.*
> *(1 Kings.8.12-13)*

Solomon has attained the level of Being represented by 'Sol', the Sun, his proper place in the soul's hierarchy, as his name implies. He has recreated himself into a Temple, a fitting place for God to dwell, and the *Shechinah* has descended and entered Her Temple.

Solomon's dedication of the Temple consists of a prophetic prayer of supplication to the Lord, on behalf of himself and all of Israel, asking the Lord to pardon and forgive their sins. This is then followed by the ritual of repentance, the *sacrifice* (from the Hebrew *korban,* which means 'to come near', to elevate oneself spiritually and draw closer to God.)

> *When they sin against You – for there is no one*
> *who does not sin – and You are angry with them*
> *and deliver them to the enemy, and their captors*
> *carry them off to an enemy land, near or far;*
> *and then they take it to heart in the land to*
> *which they have been carried off, and they*
> *repent and make supplication to You ... saying,*
> *"We have sinned, we have acted perversely, we*
> *have acted wickedly," and they turn back to You*
> *with all their heart and soul...,*
> *oh, give heed in Your heavenly abode to their*
> *prayer and supplication, uphold their cause,*
> *and pardon Your people who have sinned*
> *against You and all the transgressions*
> *that they have committed against You.*
> *(1 Kings.8.46-50)*

After Solomon's prayer, "The king and all Israel with him offered sacrifices before the Lord. Solomon offered 22,000 oxen and 120,000 sheep as sacrifices of well-being to the Lord." Then the king and all his people held a celebratory Feast that lasted for fourteen days.

All was well. This was the pinnacle of the history of ancient Israel. The nation was united under the wisest of kings, there was phenomenal prosperity, there was peace on all sides, and God was dwelling amongst them.

The necessary reaction awaited.

After the feast, God appeared to Solomon a second time, as He had in the dream in Gibeon, and told Solomon that He had "heard the prayer and supplication which you offered to Me. I consecrate this House which you have built and I set My name there forever."

> *As for you, if you walk before Me*
> *as your father David walked before Me,*
> *wholeheartedly and with uprightness...,*
> *then I will establish your throne of kingship*
> *over Israel forever.... But if you*
> *or your descendants turn away from Me...*
> *then I will sweep Israel off the land I gave them.*
> *(1 Kings.9.4-7)*

Solomon's prayer, and God's warning, will prove prophetic not only for the nation of Israel, which will soon be conquered and exiled from the Promised Land, but for Solomon himself, who is about to succumb to Temptations and is going to 'fall'.

Solomon did not just build a home for God. He built himself a home as well, an opulent and luxurious palace to celebrate his own power and glory. Solomon spent seven years building a House for God. But he spent thirteen years building a house for himself.

As described in the Bible, Solomon's palace was much larger, more architecturally complex, and more magnificent than the Temple. According to the legends, his throne alone was like nothing ever seen before or since. It was made of ivory and covered with fine gold, inlaid with marble, and studded with rubies, pearls, and emeralds. It had six steps, and upon each one there were two golden lions and two golden eagles, in addition to carvings of an ox, a leopard, a wolf, a hawk, a falcon, a dove – and of course a peacock, the symbol of pride. Over the seat was a golden candlestick, with golden lamps and carvings of pomegranates and lilies. But most remarkable of all, the throne was actually a mechanical (or perhaps magical) device – when Solomon set foot on the base, the golden beasts would take hold of him and lift him up to his seat at the top, where the eagle would place the crown upon his head.

"At the end of the twenty years during which Solomon constructed the two buildings", the Bible now tells us, he gave King Hiram of Tyre a gift to thank him for all the help he had given. The present consisted of twenty towns in the region of Galilee. "But when Hiram came from Tyre to inspect the towns that Solomon had given him, he was not pleased with them. 'My brother,' he said, 'what sort of towns are these you have given me?' So they were named Cabul, as is still the case." The word *cabul* means desolate, empty, dirty, 'as nothing'. So Solomon, the richest king in the world, in exchange for twenty years of service, has given his friend virtually nothing.

Solomon had been filled with arrogance and pride regarding his own greatness, his riches, and his wisdom, and as a result he would soon fall from the heights of glory to the depths of misery. The palace and throne indicate his complete surrender to self-importance. The empty gift to Hiram indicates the overwhelming greed that had overtaken him, such that he was not willing to part with any of his riches. Now the Queen of Sheba comes to visit, to examine his wisdom, "to test him with hard questions."

Solomon had answers for all her questions;
there was nothing that the king did not know,
nothing to which he could not
give her an answer. (1 Kings.10.3)

The Queen was "left breathless" by all this wisdom. "I did not believe the reports until I came and saw with my own eyes that not even half had been told to me; your wisdom and wealth surpass the reports that I heard."

But is this truly 'wisdom'? Socrates would spend a lifetime struggling to recognize and to bear that he really knew nothing at all, but for Solomon "there was nothing that the king did not know." There was not a single question for which he was not ready with a quick answer. This is hardly the open and humble state of the soul in which one may cross over into the divine realm and be welcomed home by God.

The Queen of Sheba, personifying the Sacred Feminine, could do nothing to help him. All she could do was to give his ego what it foolishly thought it wanted.

She presented the king with one hundred
and twenty talents of gold, and a large
quantity of spices, and precious
stones..... Then she and her attendants
left and returned to her own land
(1 Kings.10.10-13)

On the eastern shores of the Jordan River, Moses had given some very specific Teachings regarding the future kings of Israel: a king, Moses explained, must not overly concern himself with worldly values: "he shall not keep many horses .... And he shall not have many wives, lest his heart go astray; nor shall he amass silver and gold to excess."

Solomon had most certainly amassed silver and gold to excess. The Bible also says that he owned 12,000 horses. But the final straw in the downfall of Solomon was something else:

> *King Solomon loved many foreign women in*
> *addition to Pharaoh's daughter – Moabite,*
> *Ammonite, Edomite, Phoenician, and Hittite*
> *women, from the nations of which the Lord*
> *had said to the Israelites, "None of you shall*
> *join them and none of them shall join you,*
> *lest they turn your heart away to follow their*
> *gods." Such Solomon clung to and loved.*
> *(1 Kings.11.1-2)*

In fact, Solomon had no less than "seven hundred royal wives and three hundred concubines." And just as God had warned, "In his old age, his wives turned away Solomon's heart after other gods, and he was not as wholeheartedly devoted to the Lord his God as his father David had been."

Solomon's foreign 'wives', of course, symbolize lower emotions, lower influences, with which the ascending soul of an enlightened initiate (whether male or female) is no longer supposed to mix. The 'other gods' are various objects of desire in this world, desires that have to be sacrificed and transformed into unqualified desire for God. But Solomon turned away, and he "went after" *Ashtoreth* ('riches'), and *Chemosh* ('taking'), and *Molech* ('power'), and other abominations. He even built shrines and temples (within his soul) for these gods, and he worshipped and sacrificed ('drew near') to these so-called 'deities'. These, of course, are the idols that still continue to spoil our souls.

The Lord was incensed. "Because you are guilty of this," He said, "I will tear the kingdom away from you...." The Lord then raised up adversaries to Solomon (the

Hebrew word for 'adversary' is '*satan*'): Hadad the Edomite challenged him from the east; Rezon, the king of Damascus, challenged him from the north; worst of all, his friend Jeroboam, a fellow Israelite of the northern tribe of Ephraim, "raised his hand against the king." He did this because the prophet Ahijah told Jeroboam that the Lord had said: "I am about to tear the kingdom out of Solomon's hands, and I will give you ten tribes."

Solomon tried to put Jeroboam to death, but he fled to Egypt and remained there safely until the king's death.

It was 928 BCE. In Greece, Homer's *Iliad* was being written down. In Assyria, new dreams of empire were awakening. In Israel, a new civil war was brewing.

> *The length of Solomon's reign in Jerusalem,*
> *over all Israel, was forty years.*
> *Solomon slept with his fathers*
> *and was buried in the city of his father David;*
> *and his son Rehoboam succeeded him as king.*
> *(1 Kings.11.42-43)*

CHAPTER THREE

Fall and Exile

In the wake of Solomon's fall, the kingdom (and symbolically, the soul as well) quickly collapsed. First, the nation split in two, and for a hundred years there was civil strife between the nation of Judah and the nation of Israel. Throughout these years the various kings and prophets were constantly at odds with each other and internal disorder reigned. Eventually, the kingdom descended into utter fragmentation and dispersal, and all the people were exiled from the Promised Land and carried off into captivity. The great majority would sink into oblivion and disappear from history forever.

⁕⁕⁕

When Solomon's son Rehoboam first became a king, it was only over the southern division of Judah. Like Solomon and David before him, Rehoboam had to travel north to Israel and garner their support as well. So he went to the city of Shechem and was met by tribal leaders who began the meeting by presenting him with various complaints. The northern tribes were ready to accept Rehoboam as their king, they said, but only if he agreed to certain conditions: Solomon had taxed them heavily and forced them to labor on his building projects, and they wanted assurances from Rehoboam that he would now lighten their burden. Rehoboam took counsel with his advisors, and the elders told him he should placate the northerners and speak to them kindly, thus earning their friendship and gratitude. But his younger advisers and friends told him not to bow to their pressure: instead, he should threaten the northerners in order to keep them in line.

Unfortunately, Rehoboam followed the advice of his young friends. After ending the meeting on a sour note, he sent his general, Adoram, to conscript more laborers, "but all Israel pelted him to death with stones. Thereupon King Rehoboam hurriedly mounted his chariot and fled to Jerusalem. Thus Israel revolted against the House of David…" The chieftains then summoned Jeroboam, and made him king over Israel.

Rehoboam quickly mustered 180,000 soldiers from the tribes of Judah, so that they could go into battle with the tribes of Israel and restore his kingship. But the Lord spoke to the prophet Shemaiah (his name means 'hears and obeys God'), and Shemaiah repeated God's words to Rehoboam:

"You shall not set out to make war on your kinsmen the Israelites. Let every man return to his home, for this thing has been brought about by Me." (1 Kings.12.24)

So Rehoboam and his soldiers turned back, and Jeroboam fortified Shechem and the surrounding region. The nation was split asunder.

Jeroboam was a pious man, a wise scholar who had earlier been on excellent terms with Solomon. But power corrupts, and it would quickly prove to be his doom.

The city of Jerusalem, and the Temple, were sacred to citizens of both kingdoms. Pilgrims from the north would still travel to Jerusalem in the south to worship and sacrifice in the Temple. Jeroboam worried that this would eventually turn the hearts of the northerners back toward Judah and the House of David: "they will kill me," he said to himself, "and go back to King Rehoboam of Judah." So Jeroboam, out of a combination of fear and audacity, built two new Temples in his realm. And that was only the beginning.

So the king took counsel and made two
golden calves. He said to the people, "You
have been going up to Jerusalem long
enough. This is your god, O Israel, who
brought you up from the land of Egypt!"
(1 Kings.12.28)

The Lord, incensed of course, declared, "You have acted worse than all those who preceded you.... I will sweep away the House of Jeroboam utterly, as dung is swept away."

Jeroboam reigned twenty-two years;
then he slept with his fathers,
and his son Nadab succeeded him as king.
(1 Kings.14.20)

There now follows a terrible period in biblical history. For more than two centuries the dual nations of Judah and Israel were ruled by dozens of kings, and nearly each one is described in the Bible as being worse than the last one: they built shrines and altars to various 'gods', they intermarried with foreigners, they warred with each other, they usurped and slaughtered each other with endless intrigues and bloody assassinations. Throughout this disintegration, however, some 'light' still remained: wise Prophets raged against the Kings. But they were almost uniformly ridiculed or ignored.

The greatest of these prophets was Elijah, who lived during the reign of the northern King Ahab and his detestable Phoenician wife, Queen Jezebel, who murdered prophets, worshipped Baal, and sacrificed children to the fire god Moloch.

When he first appears in the story, Elijah is telling Ahab, "As the Lord lives, the God of Israel whom I serve, there will be no dew or rain except at my bidding." A terrible drought began immediately, and Elijah went into hiding to avoid the wrath of Ahab, who blamed him personally. Dew and rain represent spiritual sustenance sent by God to feed the soul. Baal was considered a god of fresh water, and those Israelites who fell into this sort of idolatry were 'fed' by, and gave credit to, Baal. When Moses was teaching on the banks of the Jordan, he had said that so long as the Israelites continued to love the Lord with all their "heart and soul, I will grant the rain for your land in season.... Take care not to be lured away to serve other gods and bow to them. For the Lord's anger will flare up against you, and He will shut up the skies so that there will be no rain...."

Since King Ahab wished to find and destroy him, God told Elijah to go to a certain widow whom God had designated to protect him, who would provide him with food and water during the drought. When he came to her and asked for a little water and bread, the woman answered that she had only enough flour and oil for one last meal for herself and her small son: "we shall eat it," she said, "and then we shall die." But Elijah told her not to be afraid, for God had promised that her jar of flour and jug of oil would not run out until the drought was ended. The miracle came true, and Elijah remained with the widow and her son. She had the prophet stay in the 'upper chamber' of their home. (The Sacred Feminine, in the guise of the Queen of Sheba, had not been able to help Solomon ascend to the 'upper chamber'. But now She is able to help and protect Elijah.)

After a while, the son became very ill "until he had no breath left in him." Elijah took the boy in his arms and brought him to the upper chamber. "He cried to the Lord and said, 'O Lord my God, will You bring calamity upon this widow whose guest I am, and let her son die?'" Elijah "stretched out over the child three times, and cried out to

50

the Lord saying, 'O Lord my God, let this child's life return to his body!'"

The Lord heard Elijah's plea; the
child's life returned to his body,
and he revived. (1 Kings.17.22)

"Now I know that you are a man of God," the widow says to him, "and that the word of the Lord is truly in your mouth."

In the third year of the drought, Elijah sent a message to Ahab and told him to bring all of Israel, including the hundreds of new priests of Baal, and meet him on Mount Carmel where he was going to conduct a great contest between Baal and the Lord. Ahab agreed, and when everyone arrived, Elijah told the priests of Baal to bring two bulls for sacrifice, to slaughter them and lay them out on wood, but not to light any fire yet. Then he challenged them:

"You will then invoke your god by name,
and I will invoke the Lord by name;
and let us agree:
the god who responds with fire,
that one is God."
And all the people answered, "Very good!"
(1 Kings.18.24)

The priests of Baal prepared their bull, and then shouted the name of Baal "from morning until noon, shouting, 'O Baal, answer us!'"

"When noon came, Elijah mocked them, saying,
"Shout louder! After all, he is a god.
But he may be in conversation,

he may be detained,
or he may be on a journey,
or perhaps he is asleep and will wake up!"
(1 Kings.18.27)

So they shouted louder, and kept raving until evening, but nothing happened.

When they finally gave up, Elijah prepared his offering, and even poured water all over and around it – Baal was supposedly the god of fresh water. When he was finished, he invoked the name of the Lord.

Then fire from the Lord descended
and consumed the burnt offering,
the wood, the stones, and the earth;
and it licked up the water that was in the trench.
(1 Kings.18.38)

The people flung themselves on their faces shouting, "The Lord alone is God, the Lord alone is God." Elijah then told them to seize the prophets of Baal, and he slaughtered them right there.

The rains (the Lord's Truths) now came, and the drought was over.

The stories of Elijah come to an end after he replaces himself on the initiatory ladder and appoints Elisha as his successor, just as Moses appointed Joshua as his successor. Together, the two prophets then journeyed to the Jordan River. Elijah struck the river with his cloak, and the waters parted so that they crossed on dry land. As they were approaching the far side, Elijah said to Elisha, "Tell me what I can do for you before I am taken from you." Elisha asked that twice as much of Elijah's Spirit pass to him. This was a difficult request, Elijah responded. But if Elisha was prepared, i.e., if the Eye of his Soul was fully awake and open, if he could *'see'*, then it would be just as he had requested: "If you see me as I am being taken from you, this will be granted to you; if not, it will not."

As they kept on walking and talking,
a fiery chariot with fiery horses suddenly
appeared and separated one from the other;
and Elijah went up to heaven in a whirlwind.
Elisha saw it, and he cried out.
"Oh, father, father!
Israel's chariots and horsemen!"
(2 Kings.2.11-12)

When he could no longer see him, Elisha picked up Elijah's cloak and walked back to the banks of the Jordan. He struck the waters with the cloak and they parted, and he crossed back over. Other prophets and disciples saw him, and they exclaimed, "The spirit of Elijah has settled on Elisha!" Then they came to meet him, and bowed low to the ground.

According to the legends, Elijah goes on living for all time. This is to be expected, for Elijah was not a mortal man: he was actually the angel Sandalphon, the angel of the Sun who weaves the prayers of mankind into garlands for the Lord's Crown. He had asked God's permission to abide temporarily on earth during a dark time, so that he could teach God's Truth. Even after his ascension, he continues to have relations with humanity, being ever a helper in need, and there are many tales of his interventions in the affairs of the world.

Even more importantly, the Hebrew legends say that it will be Elijah's mission to prepare the world for the coming of the Messiah. The prophet will return to the earth, he will induce lost souls to repent and he will bring harmony and peace to the world, for all conflicts and differences of opinion must be removed from the path of the Messiah. Elijah's final act will be the execution of God's command to slay the Evil One, and thus banish evil forever.

Like his predecessor, Elisha was a healer as well as a prophet. His stories are filled with familiar symbols and images. For example:

1) He responds to the plight of a poor woman who has only one remaining jug of oil, and is about to have her sons seized by creditors and made into slaves. Elisha miraculously causes the jug to continue filling so many vessels with oil that these could all be sold and all her debts repaid;

2) Another woman had her husband prepare the 'upper chamber' of their house as a place for Elisha to stay whenever he visited their town. Her husband was old and she had no child, but Elisha predicted that a son would be born to her the following year. Later, the child died, but Elisha came to the house, lay on top of the boy, and breathed into his mouth. The body turned warm, and the child opened his eyes and was revived;

3) He healed a leper by having the man bathe seven times in the Jordan River;

4) A man gave Elisha twenty loaves of barley bread. Elisha said, "Give it to the people and let them eat." His attendant replied, "How can I set this before a hundred men?" But Elisha said "They shall eat and have some left over." So

Elisha fed a multitude with twenty loaves of bread, and some was left over;

5) Once he and his disciples were felling trees by the Jordan to build a home. An iron ax head accidentally fell into the water and sank. Elisha caused it to float to the surface and it was retrieved;

6) Sometime after Elisha's death, another man was being buried near his cave. Suddenly, the mourners were attacked by a band of Moabites. In the confusion, they threw the man's corpse into the burial cave of Elisha. When the body touched Elisha's bones, the man came back to life and left the cave.

An interesting thing about the miracle stories of Elisha, who followed in the wake of Elijah and whose name means 'lamb of God', is that he typically acts on his own authority, without needing to invoke the Lord. Similar miracle stories, and a similar authority, will be found in the stories about Jesus that are told in the New Testament.

The kings, in the meantime, endlessly obsessed with their plots and their murders and their idolatry, continued to rule for several more generations: King Joash of Judah "did what was pleasing to the Lord, but not like his ancestor David"; King Jehoash of Israel "marched on Jerusalem…. He carried off all the gold and silver and all the vessels that were in the House of the Lord…."; King Azariah of Judah "did what was pleasing to the Lord, just as his father Amaziah had done. However, the [idolatrous] shrines were not removed"; King Zechariah of Israel "did what was displeasing to the Lord, as his fathers had done"; and so on and so forth, until the year 722 BCE, when the Assyrians, under Sargon II, after many years of war, overran the northern Kingdom of Israel, and deported all its citizenry throughout the Assyrian Empire. The Ten Tribes were dispersed, reabsorbed, and disappeared.

This, we are told, was the only possible response to two centuries of blasphemy, hatred, idolatry, and carnage.

The southern Kingdom of Judah lasted another hundred and thirty-four years. Its history was similar to the northern kingdom, though there were somewhat fewer kings, and less palace intrigue and violence. And unlike the great variety of northern dynasties, all of Judah's kings were descendants of the royal House of David.

In 640 BCE, Josiah became king of Judah. Unlike all the rest of them, we are told, he "did what was pleasing to the Lord and he followed all the ways of his ancestor David; he did not deviate to the right or to the left."

In the eighteenth year of his reign, the Temple was being repaired by "the carpenters, the laborers, and the masons." During the repairs, the high priest Hilkiah "found a scroll of the Teaching in the House of the Lord." The scroll was brought to King Josiah and read to him. When the king heard the words of Moses' Teaching, he rent his clothes. He immediately sent messengers to the prophetess Huldah, asking her to inquire of the Lord on his behalf and the people's behalf, for "great indeed must be the wrath of the Lord that has been kindled against us, because our fathers did not obey the words of this scroll to do all that has been prescribed for us." Huldah replied that the Lord indeed *was* incensed, and was going to bring a terrible disaster to Judah, for "My wrath is kindled against this place and it shall not be quenched." However, because Josiah's "heart was softened and you humbled yourself before the Lord," Huldah said that Josiah himself would not have to see the desolation and the curse, but would be gathered to his fathers before it occurred.

At the king's summons, all the elders of
Judah and Jerusalem assembled before him.
The king went up to the House of the Lord,
together with all the men of Judah and all
the inhabitants of Jerusalem, and the priests
and prophets – all the people, young and
old. And he read to them the entire text of
the covenant scroll which had been found in
the House of the Lord.... And all the people
entered into the covenant.
(2 Kings.23.1-3)

Josiah then ordered that all objects of Baal and other gods be taken out of the Temple and burned outside of Jerusalem. All worship of Baal was suppressed. All the shrines that were built outside of the Temple were destroyed, and their priests were slain. Josiah also "did away with the necromancers and the mediums, the idols and the fetishes – all the detestable things that were to be seen in the land of Judah and Jerusalem." The king then commanded his people, "Offer the passover sacrifice to the Lord your God as described in this scroll of the covenant." There had not been a Passover sacrifice since the days of Solomon.

As regards Josiah, we are told:

There was no king like him before
who turned back to the Lord
with all his heart and soul and might,
in full accord with the Teaching of Moses;
nor did any like him arise after him.
(2 Kings.23.25)

The more likely version, the one most scholars accept, is that Josiah and his close followers, in order to initiate reforms and perhaps even save the struggling remains of the Hebrew nation, wove together a new Scroll from various documents that had been written over the years in both kingdoms, and then brought out this Scroll with great fanfare, telling the people that it had been 'discovered' hidden within the Temple, and that it contained the authentic word of God as written down by Moses himself. The scroll, now known as the Book of *Deuteronomy*, was thus canonized, and the setting down of the Holy Bible was begun.

When discussing the Freemason's myth of the murder of CHiram Abiff, we noted that in times of war and upheaval there is a terrible risk that real Truth and real Hope might be lost, possibly for a very long time or even forever, unless it is preserved and protected – perhaps by a 'secret society' – pending a safer and more favorable moment in time. Josiah and the priests who worked with him were undoubtedly just such a society, a spiritual School that took upon itself the task of preserving the great wisdom of the Hebrew tradition, in the face of the destruction of their culture which they knew was fast approaching. They put together the 'Teachings of Moses', assuring that this wisdom would be studied and preserved, and would go into exile with the people of Judah. The ten tribes of Israel simply vanished from history. But, at least in part because of the efforts of the School of Josiah, the Hebrew people of the kingdom of Judah, and their great wisdom teaching, survived the exile, and many of them eventually returned to Jerusalem and rebuilt the holy city.

After the death of Josiah, several more kings reigned in Judah, but most were of little note. Assyria, in the meantime, was vanquished by Babylonia. Around the year 600 BCE, Jehoiachin became king of Judah, and one final time a king "did what was displeasing to the Lord, just as his father had done."

At that time, the troops of
King Nebuchadnezzar of Babylon
marched against Jerusalem,
and the city came under siege.... Thereupon
King Jehoiachin of Judah...
surrendered to the king of Babylon....
He exiled all of Jerusalem....
Indeed, Jerusalem and Judah
were a cause of anger for the Lord,
so that He cast them out of His presence.
(2 Kings.24.10-20)

The Temple was destroyed. The Promised Land was lost. The soul was dispersed. But the efforts of Josiah had ensured that a new story of ascent could someday begin again.

CHAPTER FOUR

Persia

Within a hundred years, the mighty Babylonian Empire, like Assyria before it, was no more. The forces of Persia completely overran it in 539 BCE. The Persians then did something quite surprising. They told the Judeans (or 'Jews', which is how the word evolved in English) that they could leave Babylon and return to their homeland. In the first year of the reign of King Cyrus of Persia, according to *Second Chronicles*:

> *[T]he Lord roused the spirit of King Cyrus*
> *of Persia to issue a proclamation*
> *throughout his realm by word of mouth and*
> *in writing, as follows: "Thus said King*
> *Cyrus of Persia: The Lord God of Heaven*
> *has given me all the kingdoms of the earth,*
> *and has charged me with building Him a*
> *House in Jerusalem, which is in Judah. Any*
> *one of you of all His people, the Lord his*
> *God be with him and let him go up.*
> *(2 Chron.36.22-23)*

But during the previous century, life in their new land had actually become quite comfortable for most of the exiles. So when Cyrus announced that the Jews could return to the devastated land of their ancestors, only a minority was interested in doing so. Those who chose to return, mostly the poorer and less fortunate of the Jews residing in Babylon, began to rebuild the city of Jerusalem and the Temple, and they started a new life as a vassal state of the Persian Empire.

Years before, when the Assyrians first exiled the ten northern tribes *out* of Israel, leaving behind only a few peasants, they brought other captive peoples *into* Israel. These people were mostly settled in Samaria, and thus became known as Samaritans. Over time, the Samaritans adopted much of the Jewish way of life, but they never did so completely. As a result, the returning exiles did not really accept them as Jews, and the Samaritans were resentful.

Now, as the returning Jews began rebuilding their Temple, the disgruntled Samaritans sent a message to Persia threatening that if the Jews were allowed to build it the Samaritans would rebel. As a result, Persian permission to build the Temple was withdrawn, and eighteen years went by before they were allowed to begin again.

During these eighteen years, the story of Queen Esther, the basis of the Purim Festival, took place. This story, which does not seem to be based on any actual historical event (after all, the Persian Empire was exceedingly tolerant toward its ethnic minorities), is a tale of courage and daring, and it also provides a wonderful comic caricature of life in the Persian Court, while providing the Jewish tradition with a *raison d'etre* for a most untypical holiday. Purim, like the great party scene with which the story begins, is a wild, bawdy, carnivalesque celebration, replete with masquerades, comedic theater, thunderous noisemaking, and – if one obeys the instructions that are given in the Talmud – drinking to excess.

In the third year of his reign, King Ahasuerus of Persia held a lavish celebration. His halls were filled with gold and silver, food and wine. The party lasted one hundred and eighty days for his nobles, princes, and soldiers, and another seven days for all the other men, great or small, who lived in the royal city. His wife, Queen Vashti, held a similar celebration for the women.

Everyone drank to their heart's content from golden goblets. On the seventh day, when Ahasuerus was merry with wine, he ordered Queen Vashti to appear at his banquet so that he might show off her beauty. She was told to wear her beautiful crown. Some legends suggest that Ahasuerus meant she should wear only her crown. However that may be, Vashti refused to come and the king was very wroth. He asked his advisors what he should do.

The King's advisors said that Vashti had wronged not only the king, but all the men of the empire, even those in the most distant provinces, since word would quickly spread regarding the Queen's disobedience – and this, if left unpunished, would inspire other wives to disobey their husbands and hold them in contempt. Therefore, the king must banish Vashti and find a new queen.

Ahasuerus did as they suggested. To choose the new queen, they advised him to have all the fair young virgins of the empire gathered together in the royal city for a beauty contest. The maiden who most pleased the king would be named the new queen.

One of the contestants was Esther, a lovely Jewish girl who was orphaned at a young age and was being raised by her elder cousin, Mordecai, a descendant of King Saul.

Each of the contestants spent a full year preparing for their meeting with the king: six months of anointing with oil of myrrh, and six months with other sweet ointments of women. Mordecai, during these months, spent his days pacing in front of the castle. At his request, Esther did not reveal to anyone that she was Jewish.

When the time came at last for her presentation to the king, Esther found favor in Ahasuerus' eyes, and he made her his new wife and queen in the seventh year of his reign.

Now it happened at this time that two of the king's chamberlains, Bigthan and Teresh, plotted to kill the king. Mordecai, who was always hanging around the grounds of the palace, learned of their plot: he informed Queen Esther, and Esther reported it to the king in Mordecai's name. The king ordered the chamberlains to be hanged.

Shortly after this, Ahasuerus chose an advisor named Haman to be his senior minister, above all the other princes of the land. Haman was a descendant of the Amalekite king, Agag, whom King Saul had long ago spared: this had cost Saul the kingdom.

Haman demanded complete loyalty from everyone in the king's service, and ordered all to bow down to him. But Mordecai refused, giving as an excuse that he was forbidden from bowing down to Haman by his Jewish faith (by which he was saying that he would never bow to an Amalekite). This angered Haman, and he determined to destroy not only Mordecai, but all the Jews in the Persian Empire.

Haman and his servants cast "pur" – that is, they cast lots – to determine the most propitious time to annihilate the Jews. The lots chose the month of Adar. Haman then went to King Ahasuerus and told him that there was a people, called Jews, scattered throughout his kingdom, who kept their own laws and did not obey the king's laws. He asked Ahasuerus for permission to destroy them, and offered the king ten thousand talents of silver (to be confiscated from these enemies). Ahasuerus, never quite sure of what to do and always at the mercy of his advisors, agreed to Haman's request and promptly went back to his drinking and partying. Meanwhile, a proclamation was sent throughout the kingdom declaring that the empire's officials must slay all the Jews, young and old, women and children, on the thirteenth day of Adar, and take all their riches for booty.

News of the decree spread throughout the kingdom, and the Jews became greatly agitated. Mordecai urged Esther to plead with the king to save the lives of her people. Esther reminded Mordecai that no one could come before the king unbidden: the punishment was death, unless the king held out his scepter to the uninvited visitor as an act of pardon. Mordecai reminded her that if the proclamation was not rescinded she would die anyway. And who knows, he said, perhaps she had attained her royal position just to avert such a crisis. So after telling Mordecai to have the people fast for three days on her behalf, Esther summoned all of her courage and went before the king.

As soon as he saw her, Ahasuerus extended his golden scepter. He then asked her what request she had, adding that he would give her whatever she wished. She responded that she wished to invite the king and Haman to a feast she was preparing.

The king summoned Haman to hurry along, and they went to the feast. Again Ahasuerus asked Esther if she had a request. She seemed on the verge of telling him what she really wanted, but suddenly interrupted herself and merely invited them to another feast the following night. Tomorrow, she said, she would make her request.

All the next day, while waiting for the second feast with Queen Esther, Haman – who now believed himself the recipient of two great honors – was in a wonderful mood. That is, until he ran into Mordecai, who again refused to bow down and thereby spoiled all his gaiety. Nonetheless, he controlled himself and went home, where he bragged to his wife and friends about all the honors he was receiving, including two back-to-back invitations to dine alone with the royal couple. And yet, he bemoaned, all of this meant nothing every time he saw that insolent Jew Mordecai sitting out by the palace gate, refusing to bow to him.

To cheer him up, his wife suggested that he build a stake in the backyard, 50 cubits high (about the size of a seven-story building), and get permission to impale Mordecai on it. Haman thought it a splendid idea, and had the stake put up.

That night, as fate would have it, Ahasuerus had trouble sleeping. So to pass the time, he had his Book of Records brought in and read to him. In it was a report of the two chamberlains, Bigthan and Teresh, who had plotted to murder him, and how his life had been saved by Mordecai. "What honor has been conferred upon Mordecai?" he asked. "Nothing at all has been done for him," was the reply. So the king, always looking for an advisor to tell him what to do, asked, "Who is in the palace tonight?" And it happened that Haman had just entered the palace, hoping to get a chance to ask the king for permission to impale Mordecai. "Tell him to come in!" said Ahasuerus.

When Haman came in he did not even get a chance to ask his question, because immediately the king said to him, "Haman, what should be done for a man whom the king desires to honor?" Haman smiled to himself. Here, apparently, was yet a third great honor coming his way: "Whom should the king wish to honor," he thought, "more than me?" So he advised the king that such a man should be dressed in the king's robes, put upon the king's horse, and paraded through the city so that all could pay him honor. "Excellent," said Ahasuerus. "Now quickly, get the robes and the horse and do all of this for Mordecai the Jew who sits at the palace gate. Do everything exactly as you have proposed!"

Haman, utterly humiliated, did as the oblivious king had ordered him. He then staggered home and told the whole sad story to his wife, who seemed to intuit that his doom was upon him.

He pulled himself together somehow, and when the king's servants came to fetch him he dragged himself to the second feast with Esther.

As they reclined at dinner, the king again asked his wife, "What is it you wish, Queen Esther? Whatever it is it shall be granted." This time she responded, "Your Majesty, what I wish is for you to spare my life, and the lives of my people. For I am a Jew, the cousin of Mordecai, and we have been told that all of us are to be massacred." This news astonished the king, who demanded to know who had dared to threaten such a thing. "Our enemy," she replied, "is this very Haman!" At this, the king actually stormed out of the room, and the terrified Haman fell upon the couch where Esther was reclining and pleaded with her for his life. Ahasuerus came back in, and seeing Haman on the couch with his wife he cried out, "Do you man to ravish the queen in my own palace?" At this, one of the servants said, "And what is more, he has built a fifty cubit stake at his house, upon which he intends to impale Mordecai!"

"Impale him on it!" the king ordered. And thus did Haman meet his end.

Ahasuerus then told Esther that his previous royal decree against the Jews could not be legally annulled, but what he could do was to issue an additional decree, giving the Jews the right to defend themselves against anyone who attacked them. So on the 13th of Adar, five hundred attackers and Haman's ten sons were killed in the royal city, and throughout the empire another 75,000 enemies were slain. Mordecai was then given Haman's property, and his position in the Court.

His first act was to charge his people with the obligation to observe the festival of Purim each year, a celebration of the transformation of grief to joy, with feasting and merrymaking, and an occasion for making gifts to the poor.

According to Jewish lore, the Persian king, Darius II, was the son of Queen Esther and King Ahasuerus [possibly Xerxes I]. Whatever the truth of his lineage, Darius II at last allowed the Jews in Palestine to go back to rebuilding their Temple.

The Second Temple was completed around 515 BCE, but it was hardly the same. The Holy of Holies stood empty: the Ark of the Covenant, with the Tablets of the Law and the Mercy Seat for the *Shechinah*, was gone. Some stories say that the Ark was stolen by the Babylonians. Others believe that King Josiah, aware of the looming disaster, had hidden the Ark in the Temple Mount – that is, somewhere deep within Mount Moriah. (The Second Temple was a humble edifice compared to its progenitor. Many years later, around 30 BCE, Herod the Great would refurbish it into a spectacular structure, but it would still be spiritually empty).

Back in the Persian Empire, word came that the settlers in Jerusalem were leaderless and suffering from low morale. Ezra, a high-born priest, scholar, and scribe in the Persian court, received permission in 458 BCE to lead a second exodus of eighteen hundred Jews back to Judea. His self-defined mission was (1) to preserve the nation by absolutely forbidding intermarriage; (2) to reinstate the Mosaic Law; and (3) to raise the spiritual consciousness of the people wherever they might live now or in the future, by writing down and preserving the entire wisdom Teaching.

Ezra put together a new spiritual School, known to us as the Great Assembly, which included 120 members including the last of the Prophets (Haggai, Zechariah, and Malachi), great sages, the chief architect of the Temple (Nechemia), High Priests, and Elders. During the Second Temple period, it was the Great Assembly that wove together the complete written Torah (the Five Books of

Moses – *Genesis, Exodus, Leviticus,* and *Numbers,* plus Josiah's *Deuteronomy),* as well as gathering other books for the Hebrew Bible. They also began writing down many of the Oral Teachings, so that these would never be lost, in a compilation that has come to be called the Talmud. Lastly, they formalized the Jewish prayer liturgy – which was necessary now that the Ark was gone and the direct connection to God was severed.

The era in which divinely ordained Prophets, like Moses and Elijah, heard the word of God and brought it to a united Hebrew people, was passing away. With the collapse of the kingdom, the loss of the Ark, and with Jews now dispersed throughout various communities around the world (i.e., the 'Diaspora', which means *dispersion),* the task of spiritual leadership fell on the shoulders of a new class of teachers, 'men of learning' called Rabbis. The work of the Great Assembly bridged the gap between the age of Prophetic Judaism and the age of Rabbinic Judaism.

Meanwhile, the Persians had continued on their mission of world conquest, and had eventually found themselves entrenched in several wars with a new power rising in the west. In 481 BCE, they were defeated by the Athenians, lost most of their Greek colonies in Asia Minor, and were driven back east. Athens soon entered its Golden Age. As Richard Hooker notes, "Flush with wealth and at peace with Persia and Sparta, the Athenians had nothing better to do...than invest it in a massive cultural flowering of art, poetry, philosophy, and architecture."[1] Greek ideas, as we shall see, will soon affect the Jews of Judea, and the whole world.

A hundred and fifty years later, Alexander the Great would completely wipe out the Persian Empire, and attempt to Hellenize the entire known world, including his new vassal state of Judah.

CHAPTER FIVE

The Greek Mind

After the execution of Socrates in 399 B.C.E., many of his disciples, including Plato*, disgusted with their fellow Athenians and fearful of further reprisals, fled from Athens. Plato began a long period of traveling, meeting and studying with priests and sages from many lands. He traveled to Sicily, Italy, and Egypt. He studied philosophy, astronomy, mathematics, and various religious systems. Finally, after twelve years of wandering and learning, he returned to Athens and founded the Academy, considered the first European university, on land he bought just outside the city walls, in a grove which was sacred to the hero Academus. Plato's Academy served as the model for institutions of higher learning until it was closed by the Emperor Justinian in 529 C.E. – almost a thousand years later.

Plato devoted his remaining years to teaching and writing. The dialogues he wrote were for the general public, but his most serious work took place in the Academy. Like all great spiritual teachings, his was fundamentally and necessarily an oral tradition.

Plato's 'Levels of Being'

A key part of Plato's philosophy was his belief in higher and lower levels of existence. In his book *Republic*, he uses the image of a 'divided line' to elucidate these different levels of existence: the lower level is the world we perceive

---

* For a much more complete discussion of the lives and ideas of Socrates and Plato, see *Return to Meaning: The American Psyche in Search of its Soul,* Andrew Cort, 2008

with our senses – the world we can see, touch, weigh, and measure. The upper level is not material, and can only be apprehended by the mind.

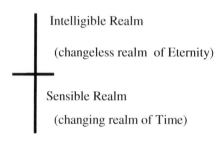

Intelligible Realm

(changeless realm of Eternity)

Sensible Realm

(changing realm of Time)

In the lower division, there are two further subdivisions. The lowest of these corresponds to shadows and reflections, i.e., the insubstantial images of substantial material things, things we only *imagine* that we see. The next segment corresponds to the material things themselves – actual visible objects, such as "the animals which we see, and everything that grows or is made."[2] Here is everything we can see and touch.

In the upper division, representing the invisible Intelligible world, there are also two divisions. The first of these is the realm of pure mental concepts, such as "geometry, arithmetic, and the kindred sciences."[3] Here we find invisible abstractions such as 'points', 'lines', and 'triangles', and the principles and axioms that relate them through *pure reason*. (These can have visible counterparts, drawings which exist in the visible world: but these drawings are only imperfect copies made of chalk or ink. The 'things themselves', the mental concepts, exist only in the invisible, intelligible, world.)

Finally, the highest level is the level of *pure ideas*, Archetypes, what Plato called the 'Forms'. Forms are essential meanings, perfect ideals, universal truths, which are only accessible to us when we have an open, awake, enlightened 'Eye of the Soul' – the highest potential faculty within the human soul. This third 'Eye' is also called *Nous*.

The highest of the Platonic Forms is 'the Good'.

For Plato, the higher the level on this scale, the more 'real' something is. Thus, the changeable world we *see* is not very real, but the changeless eternal 'Forms' are *very* real.

Consider the idea of Beauty. We might say that a woman is beautiful, a sunset is beautiful, a work of art is beautiful, or a stallion is beautiful. What *is* this quality, this "Beauty", which all these different things share in common? What is it *in itself*? What *is* 'Courage', 'Wisdom', 'Temperance', 'Justice', and the highest ideal of all, which Socrates and Plato called 'the Good'? These are objects of thought and contemplation, which have no material substance, no material reality. But according to Plato they are far more 'real' than the objects accessible to our senses, which are only copies. Just as a *drawn* triangle is only an imperfect copy of a *real, intelligible,* triangle, so the beauty of a woman is a reflection of *real* beauty, the 'Form of Beauty'. Likewise, the courage of a soldier is a reflection of the 'Form of Courage'.

Over time, all visible things will change, decay, and finally disappear. This world, the 'Below', can hardly be called 'real'. But the Forms are *outside* of time. They are in the world 'Above'. They are eternal, changeless, perfect, and perfectly real.

Aristotle

The most famous student of the Academy was Aristotle, who arrived in 366 BCE. Aristotle had been born in the north, where his father was the court physician to the King of Macedonia, Amyntas, the father of Philip, who would in turn become the father of Alexander the Great. Aristotle's parents died when he was young, and at the age of eighteen he came to Athens to study with the renowned Plato. He remained there for twenty years, until his master passed on at the age of eighty in 347 BCE. When Plato's nephew, Speusippus, was named as his uncle's successor, Aristotle and his colleague Xenocrates left the Academy for the city of Atarneus, which was ruled by another friend and former student, Hermias. There he married Hermias' niece, and then spent three years studying biology at a school Hermias had built in nearby Assus. According to legend, he spent his honeymoon collecting specimens at the seashore.

In 343 BCE, when Aristotle was forty-one, Philip was King in Macedonia. He was a leader of stunning abilities who was transforming his poor and backward country into a great power. He had tried to induce the neighboring Greek city-states to join with him in finally vanquishing their Persian enemy, but the Greeks were too suspicious of him, and were unable to overcome their own mutual animosities, so the alliance never occurred.

Now Philip invited Aristotle to come and serve as tutor to his thirteen-year-old son, and Aristotle agreed. He remained with Alexander for seven years, during which time Athens and several other Greek cities made the mistake of trying to defy Philip, and their armies were overwhelmed and forced into his service. With plenty of Greek soldiers now under his thumb, the Macedonian king finally put his long-delayed plans for the attack on Persia into place, but on the eve of the campaign he was assassinated, and Alexander came to power.

Alexander soon proved to be an even more formidable general than his father. He quickly reduced all of Greece into submission, and soon conquered Assyria, Egypt, Babylon, and at last made a clean sweep of the Persian

Empire. His tutor, in the meantime, had returned to Athens, now under Macedonian control.

Speusippus had died, and Aristotle's old friend and travel companion, Xenocrates, was now the head of the Academy. But instead of returning there, he founded a new school of his own, in another sacred grove outside the walls of Athens, evidently with funding from his famous former pupil. It was named the Lyceum. It became the chief rival of the Academy, and there Aristotle wrote and taught for many years.

His teaching method was different from his forebears. Rather than the give-and-take of Socratic dialogue, Aristotle lectured. Virtually all of his writings which survive consist of transcribed lectures and lecture notes. His extant work consists of learned treatises on logic, astronomy, physics, biology, ethics, physiology, politics, metaphysics, drama – an incredible range, and yet it is believed that three-quarters of his writings, including scores of brilliant books and dialogues, have vanished with the ages. His surviving work would nonetheless become the basis for centuries of Christian scholarship.

Aristotle Breaks With Plato

Aristotle revered Plato, but his was a more 'this-worldly' temperament. He was an empirical scientist down to the core. There could be nothing in the intellect, he asserted absolutely, that did not get there via the senses. He quickly abandoned Plato's premise of distinct levels of existence: for Aristotle, there was no purely intelligible realm of invisible Forms, since everything was on the same level, and everything was available to observation and logic. He wrote extensive criticism of Plato's theory of the Forms, denying that universal principles exist over and above particular sensible objects, or distinct from them.

Forms do exist, he believed, but not as things-in-themselves, and certainly not on some different level of Being. Instead, he brought the Forms down from the perfect bliss of unchanging eternity, and plunged them into the world of time and sense. They were more like "blueprints" or, as he called them, "potentials", but they were potentials which only existed *within* each particular material object. An acorn, for example, contained the Form of an oak tree. For this reason, it tended to move toward the goal of becoming an oak tree. It might not make it (it might be eaten by a squirrel), but if allowed to proceed to its destiny it would and could only become an oak tree, since beech trees, or other things, were not part of its 'Form'.

In Plato's view, the transcendent Forms lent purpose and meaning to the world of the senses, they provided the template for the most perfect possible world, a moving image of divine eternity. Aristotle's Forms, as 'potentials' within matter itself, were depleted of these attributes. Plato and Socrates apparently discerned much of their vast knowledge by a direct spiritual confrontation with reality, by means of an awakened *Nous*. Aristotle claimed no such ability, and without this he could only view their statements as 'unproven'. He was bothered by their assumption that a sensible object can somehow 'partake' of something else, particularly when that something else is a separate and distinct entity existing in some alleged higher world. He concluded instead that a sound foundation of knowledge must begin with the objects of the sensible world, and thus for Aristotle there was only this one level of reality.

Aristotle's Cosmology

Aristotle taught that the universe was a finite sphere with the Earth in the center. The Earth, and all its components and inhabitants, are comprised of the familiar 'four elements'. Each of these elements has a proper 'place', determined by its relative weight. This simple yet ingenious theory accounts for most of the phenomena we witness. Earth is the heaviest element, and therefore belongs at the bottom. Water is next in heaviness, and therefore, wherever it is found, it covers the earth. Air is third in heaviness, and therefore floats over the earth and water. And fire is the lightest and thus belongs above, which is why the sun and stars remain in the heavens. This concept of different types of matter having their own 'natural place' explains many basic observations of physics, such as why a dropped rock always falls to the ground and why a flame always shoots upward: they are simply drawn to their proper natural 'place'.

If these elements were left alone, he surmised, they would settle into neat concentric 'shells', surrounding each other like four layers of an onion. But their numerous motions and activities mix things up so that the layers are not so neat.

Aristotle believed that the heavens were made of a fifth element, an element that was superior to the four elements of Earth. This fifth element he called Ether. The things of the Earth were subject to change and decay, but the things made of Ether were perfect and changeless. Because of this perfect changelessness, the heavens *were* able to arrange themselves into a series of neat concentric shells.

These heavenly shells rotated around each other in perfect circles and never come to a halt. At the far limits of the universe, Aristotle could see that the world was encased within a "sphere of the fixed stars". This outermost shell (or sphere) rotates around the Earth from west to east: the stars themselves are 'fixed' within it and do not move relative to each other.

In gazing at the countless stars, however, it had long been noticed that five of them were in fact *not* 'fixed', five of them seemed to wander about at random. The Greek word for "wanderers" was *planates*. By noting how long it took these wandering bodies to complete full circuits around the Earth, early astronomers had determined the order in which they were arranged: beyond the Earth the Moon came first, then Mercury, then Venus, then the Sun, Mars, Jupiter, and Saturn. Aristotle said that each of these seven celestial bodies was contained within shells of their own that moved independently of each other. Each day their occupant would rise against a different background of stars and circle the Earth 'backwards', from east to west.

By watching the planetary movements carefully, a troubling phenomenon had been discovered. The five wanderers did not move in perfect circles! They sped up and slowed down, and sometimes they actually came to a halt, backed up, and then started moving forward again. Aristotle attempted to solve this problem by theorizing that the planets themselves do not rotate around the Earth: rather, a 'point' *within* the shell makes a perfect circle around the Earth, but the planet itself makes small, continuous circles (epicycles) around the point (like a man walking a circle around a field, while a dog keeps running in circles around him). This theory preserved the requirement that perfect heavenly bodies could only move in perfect circles, and it explains very well how an observer on Earth might see a planet change its speed and occasionally even change its direction. But applying this to the actual observed movements proved difficult, since the planets did not back up and go forward with the regularity that such a theory anticipated. Various models were tried over the centuries, all of which were variations of Aristotle's epicycles, including epicycles circling around other epicycles and all sorts of complexities. None of them quite worked. This "problem of the planets" would take almost two thousand years to be solved.

The *Unmoved Mover*

And there was still the question of why things moved *at all.*

Aristotle said that the circling motions of the etheric shells whipped up eddies and currents in the earthly shells, and this accounted for the motion of things on Earth. But why were the perfect etheric shells moving to begin with? That is, one moving shell could set the next one into motion, but what explains the *first* movement? For Aristotle, this required an "Unmoved Mover" to initiate that first movement of the first heavenly sphere.

This initial cause is found, according to Aristotle, in the one Form which he said was *not* encased in matter, the one perfect Form which served simultaneously as the initiator of all the world's motions, and as the final 'end' to which the entire universe aspires to return. In other words, the Unmoved Mover did not set things in motion by any sort of mechanical propulsion. Instead, it did so by *attraction,* as the object of *desire*, in much the same way that a beautiful woman 'moves' a man to her side.

This cause of the world's movement, Aristotle explained, is God. But as F. M. Cornford notes, "The argument demonstrating the existence of such a being is unconvincing to a modern scientific mind, and strikes a chill to the religious consciousness." Aristotle's God is merely a requirement for his mechanics. Other than being the 'Prime Mover', God plays no role in the world, nor is he even aware of its existence. His only activity is contemplation, and the only thing worthy of his contemplation is himself. Being perfect, he desires nothing, and therefore spends eternity immersed in self-contemplation. He is, however, the object of the world's desire.

Aristotle respected self-reliance above all things, and therefore his God is the epitome of self-reliance: he needs nothing, wants nothing, generates nothing. He has no need to create the world, and he has no dependence upon it. He remains in the bliss of eternal self-contemplation, and as such is 'That' toward which the world strives.

But Aristotle's God can offer no explanation as to *why* the world exists.

This theology "strikes a chill" in the religious-minded because this Being whom Aristotle describes as the goal of the world's aspiration has ceased to be an object that could possibly excite much human desire. God has been rationalized into something of no more emotional significance than a bit of 'gravitational pull'.

Socrates believed that a Divine Power must plan and order the universe for the best. When Plato turned to a consideration of the sensible external world, his science and theology met this demand. But none of this remained in Aristotle's system. God did not create the world for any good end: his influence on the world was restricted to merely causing the movements of the stars. The striving of the soul for perfection, conceived of by Socrates and expanded by Plato to include a purposeful movement of *all* Creation toward the same divine perfection, was reduced by Aristotle to a dry mechanical philosophy. If Socrates could have read Aristotle's book, *Metaphysics*, he would never have recognized the mundane outcome of the great philosophical and spiritual work that he himself had initiated.

In 323 BCE, Alexander died of a fever, and his kingdom was broken up by his various military subordinates. With the waning of Macedonian power, a wave of anti-Macedonian sentiment overtook the proud Athenians. Aristotle, who came from their land and was even the tutor of Alexander himself, felt the sting. Like Socrates, he soon found himself facing trumped up charges of impiety. But unlike Socrates, he owed no natural allegiance to the city of Athens or its laws, so he fled to his mother's native city of Chalcis, refusing to let Athens "sin twice against philosophy". There he died the following year. The great classical age of Greece was over.

CHAPTER SIX

The Second Kingdom of Judah

Following the death of Alexander, his generals divvied up the empire. The Greek city-states went to Antigonus. The northern region that stretched from Persia through Babylonia and Assyria and on to the Ionian colonies on the Aegean Sea, was taken by Seleucis. The southern region, including Egypt and Palestine, was taken by Ptolemy.

For a hundred and twenty-five years, the Ptolemies (i.e., Ptolemy I, Ptolemy II[*], etc.), ruled Palestine with a generally tolerant, hands-off attitude: as long as the Jews paid their taxes, they could govern themselves and worship however they pleased.

Their chief administrator was the High Priest who ruled in conjunction with the Assembly, and initially during this period the people thrived and prospered. But below the surface there were three great tensions. One was between the Hebrew culture and the imposed Greek culture. The second was a political tension between the Ptolemies and the Seleucids. The third was a religious difference of opinion.

The Greeks, since Alexander, expected their vassals to adopt their language, manners, customs, and ideals. Aristotle, with his emotionally barren belief in an Unmoved Mover and the isolating virtue of self-reliance, was not the

---

[*] It was Ptolemy II who compelled seventy Jewish sages to translate the Torah into Greek. The translation is known as the *Septuagint.* Ptolemy II and his Greek subjects were pleased to have another volume of human wisdom on their shelves, but the sages grieved. They knew that without the oral teachings, the Greek Torah was just another 'literary classic' that could only be read literally – as history and a description of social legislation.

only philosophy with which the Jews had to contend. Among various other alien ideas, they had to cope with the popular philosophy of Epicureanism. This distortion of the genuine ideas of Epicurus (who was actually an ascetic) encouraged a life of cynicism, in which Divinity played no role in human life, and our only purpose was to free ourselves from concerns about morality so that we could pursue a life of physical pleasure. As has always been the case, this was a very fashionable and attractive philosophy for many people, especially among the young. Between the prosperity and the pleasure, many Jews were happy to be Hellenized. In response to this, however, there was a conservative reaction among those Jews who still revered the Mosaic Law and the religious culture of their ancestors, and who maintained a firm belief that the royal line of David would one day be restored to the throne. These Jews became members of a political group known as the Hasideans.[*] The nation was soon split between pro- and anti-Hellenists.

The second tension was due to the constant fighting between the Ptolemies and the Seleucids, both of whom wanted control of the eastern Mediterranean seaboard which included Palestine. Finally, in 200 BCE the Seleucids, under Antiochus III, wrested Palestine from the Ptolemies. Still, Antiochus continued to allow the Jews freedom of worship and the right to govern themselves, and once again many people were perfectly content to be tax-paying vassals of the latest Hellenic emperor.

Antiochus soon decided that he wanted to expand his empire even further, and he marched into Egypt intending to collect more property. There, however, he ran into the latest contender for world domination, the Romans, who had only recently become the masters of all Italy and were

---

[*] Not to be confused with the *Hasidim,* a spiritual renewal movement that began in Eastern Europe in the in 18th century.

now beginning their own expansionist policy. One look at the Roman legions and Antiochus turned back.

But he still thought he might be able to defeat these upstarts if he had the help of a truly united empire behind him. So Antiochus embarked on an intense project of Hellenization throughout his realm, including placing statues of himself, as a god, everywhere. In Palestine, of course, the Jews objected to this idolatrous project, and Antiochus decided to let them be – so long as they demonstrated their continued loyalty by providing taxes and soldiers. But then Antiochus III died, and the son who soon took over, 'Antiochus Epiphanes', was not so agreeable.

The Seleucid kings would customarily appoint governors to rule their vassal states. But in the case of Palestine, which governed itself so admirably, the custom had been to appoint a High Priest who had been recommended by the people themselves. This time, the aristocratic pro-Hellenist forces in Palestine, believing it to be in their best interest to support Antiochus Epiphanes in his Hellenization program, convinced him (and very likely bribed him) to appoint one of their members, a priest named Jason, as the new High Priest. Within a year, there were Greek statues and Greek rites in the Temple. In response to this, more and more moderate Jews flocked to the anti-Hellenist Hasidean party, and the divisiveness in Palestine approached a state of civil war.

Jason, meanwhile, did not hold his job for very long. Three years later, he sent a man named Menaleus to Antiochus, in order to deliver the tributary taxes that were due to the emperor. But Menaleus betrayed him, literally outbid him, and came back as the newly appointed High Priest. Menaleus was not even a priest. The High Priesthood, which controlled the great wealth of the Temple, had became a corrupt institution for sale to the highest bidder.

In the midst of all of this, yet a third schism began to surface, this one an ideological schism between factions of religious Jews.

A priest named Zaddok taught a form of Judaism which, among other things, denied the possibility of any sort of reward or punishment in the world hereafter – in fact, Zaddok said there was *no such thing* as a 'world hereafter'. After all, there was nothing expressly written in the Torah that proclaimed such an afterlife, and Zaddok and his followers – who were known as Sadducees – read the written Torah literally: they categorically denied the validity of the Oral Torah, or the right of sages and rabbis to interpret the written word. They were religious conservatives who harkened back to a fundamentalist version of Prophetic Judaism. Yet the logical result of their insistence on 'no life hereafter' was that our first priority should be to pursue personal gratification in this one. This made the Sadducee philosophy a friendly companion of Epicureanism in particular and Hellenism in general. So even though they were religious conservatives and loyal Jews, they were politically 'enlightened' and were willing to welcome a certain amount of intrusion by modern Greek culture. (Actually, for some at least, their religious stance may have been a sham used to justify their politics. Josephus Flavius describes them as basically irreligious). The Sadducees were mostly aristocrats and priests, members of the wealthy upper class.

In response to this, a larger and more mainstream group was formed that called themselves Pharisees. The Pharisees were religious liberals: they accepted and supported the symbolic interpretations of the Oral Torah (which they believed had *also* been given to Moses when he spoke with God on Mt. Sinai), including the teachings about resurrection and the afterlife. They stressed the importance of the Synagogue, the Rabbis, and the new Prayer Liturgy, while the Sadducees stressed the importance of the Written Torah (exclusively), the Temple, and the ancient rituals of Sacrifice. The Pharisees, whose members were drawn mostly from the 'common people' such as merchants and farmers, became very punctilious in the formal observation of their version of religious law. This 'separated' them from the general populace (the name 'Pharisee' means 'Separatist'), most of whom were probably too busy just surviving to think much about either party. The Pharisees wanted the Greeks and their entire culture to get out of Palestine.

In time, the tensions between these various groups would increase, and eventually break out into open conflict.

The Chanukah Story

Antiochus Epiphanes' Hellenization project was successful in the rest of the Seleucid Empire, and even in Palestine he had his supporters. So, believing he was strong enough to face the Romans, he headed once again to Egypt. He was quickly sent packing by the Roman legions[*], and a rumor reached the Jews in Palestine that he had been killed. Members of the Hasidean party took this news as a signal that the time was ripe to purge the nation of traitorous Jewish supporters of Hellenism and desecrators of the Temple. Many were killed, and the Greek statues in the Temple were thrown over the wall and smashed.

Antiochus, however, was very much alive, and when news of the uprising reached him, right on the heels of his humiliation by Rome, he was enraged. He marched into

---

[*] In fact, the Romans declared themselves henceforth the 'Protector' of the Greek-speaking peoples, and Antiochus was forced thereafter to pay them an annual Tribute. So the citizens of Palestine were now, by some strange logic of politics, simultaneously the vassals of the Greek Seleucids while under the 'protection' of Rome.

Jerusalem, slaughtered thousands of people indiscriminately, installed new statues in the Temple, looted the Temple's wealth, and invited pagans to come to Jerusalem and settle there. Still angry, some reports say that he outlawed the Sabbath, forced Jews to sacrifice pigs to pagan gods in their own Temple, and forbade circumcision. It was a reign of terror.

In 167 BCE, in a small town near Jerusalem, a Greek official ordered an old Jewish priest named Mattathias to sacrifice a pig to the Greek gods. It would set a good example, the official said, and he promised Mattathias a handsome reward if he complied. The old priest defiantly refused, but while he was upbraiding the official a fellow Jew approached the altar and began preparing to offer the sacrifice. Mattathias, filled with a blazing anger and indignation, grabbed a sword and killed both the renegade Jew and the Greek official. He then turned to the crowd that had gathered and said, "Follow me, all of you who are for God's law and stand by the covenant!"

Those who joined Mattathias, including his five sons, hid in the hills and organized a guerrilla army led by the eldest son, Judah. Judah and his soldiers were so successful that they were given the nickname "the Hammers" – in Hebrew, "the Maccabees" – because of all the hammer blows they dealt the enemy. Though vastly outnumbered, they waged a long and bitter war which they eventually won, and the legend of the Maccabees spread throughout the empire, causing the Seleucid rulers much consternation.

Antiochus first sent a small force to stop the revolt. Judah annihilated them. Then a larger force was sent. This time, Antiochus was so confident of victory that he brought slave auctioneers with him and promised them a large supply of Jewish slaves after the battle. Again, the Maccabees were victorious.

After the third year of fighting, Judah was able to reconquer Jerusalem and chase away the Hellenist sympathizers. When the Maccabees entered the Temple, they found it desecrated, filled with pagan statues, overgrown with vegetation, and its holy implements – including the golden *Menorah* (the Candlestick) – stolen: in fact, much of the Temple's wealth had been used by the Seleucid kings to pay the Romans their tributes. Judah and his followers threw out all the idols, cleansed everything, constructed a new Menorah, and rededicated the Temple on the 25th day of the Jewish month of Kislev, in 164 BCE. But they could only find enough oil to keep the Menorah burning for one day (it was supposed to burn continuously), and it was an eight day journey to bring back and prepare a new supply of oil. Miraculously, the oil continued to burn for eight days. This miracle is still commemorated by the Festival of Lights, the Chanukah Festival, when Jews light candles on a Menorah for eight days.

The word *Chanukah* comes from the Hebrew word *chein*, which means Divine 'Grace' – i.e., God's *Light*. With God's help, the Maccabees overcame incredible odds. The candle lighting ceremony of Chanukah is meant to remind us of God's Grace and to rekindle Hope in the human heart during times of adversity.

Judah's triumph, however, was not yet complete, and there would be many more years of fighting. But in battle after battle, the Seleucids were forced to retreat. Mattathias and Antiochus Epiphanes both died during this time, and four of Mattathias' sons would eventually die in battle, including Judah Maccabee. But at last, in 143 BCE, Antiochus' successor, no longer certain of victory, tired of the endless guerrilla warfare, and feeling weak and threatened by Rome, signed a peace treaty with Mattathias' only surviving son, Simon.

The Israelite Nation was once again free.

The Hasmonean Dynasty

The new Kingdom of Judah would not be free for very long.

The elders and priests got together and named Simon to the positions of High Priest and Governor of Judah. Simon understood that to be named a *King* in Judah one had to be a descendant of David, but his heirs would quickly forget this. Although they were nicknamed "the Maccabees", the family name was *Hasmoneas*, and the kings who followed Simon would be known as the Hasmonean Dynasty.

Simon was shrewd, and he realized that both the Ptolemies and the Seleucids would be waiting for a favorable moment to attack the Jews again and retake Palestine: commercially and militarily, this gateway to the Mediterranean Sea was too valuable to ignore. To prepare for this eventuality, he signed a mutual defense pact with the Romans so that they would be obligated to help him ward off any future invasion by the Greeks.

During Antiochus Epiphanes' reign of terror, Pharisees and Sadducees alike had flocked to the banner of the anti-Hellenist Hasidean party and they had all fought alongside the Maccabees. But with the success of the revolt, there was no longer any political reason to hold these religious opponents together. Even in Simon's own family there were followers of both groups, and a classic family rift was soon set in motion.

Simon was eventually assassinated by his own son-in-law in 135 BCE, and his son, John Hyrcanus, took over. Hyrcanus got himself anointed as High Priest *and* crowned King, thus merging the two offices. From this point on, the history becomes a virtual parody of the Philosopher-King ideal, in which obvious pretenders, who have earned nothing, shatter their world and make a total disaster of the kingdom.

Hyrcanus was a Pharisee, but he quickly managed to offend and alienate this group as his interests became more and more political and secular. When some Pharisees complained that he was not following prescribed formalities of worship and behavior, he became angry. He forbade the observance of laws they had promulgated, and he switched his allegiance to the Sadducees.

Toward the end of his reign, Hyrcanus conquered several neighboring lands, including the territories of the Galileans and the Idumeans, building up the size of the Jewish state to what it was in the days of Solomon. He then did something that is virtually unheard of in the history of Judaism outside of this period: he converted these pagans to Judaism by the sword (Judaism traditionally *discourages* conversion).

When he died in 105 BCE, Hyrcanus left five sons. But although his will left the High Priesthood to his eldest son Aristobulus, it left the government to his wife. Aristobulus, however, put his mother in prison and left her there to starve. He then took over the government for himself. He also put three of his brothers in prison, and murdered the fourth. Fortunately, he himself died of illness after just one year in power.

After Aristobulus' death, his widow Alexandra had the three brothers released from prison. She managed to get the eldest, Alexander Janneus, installed as the new king, and she then married him. Alexander Janneus proved to be a violent ruler who was constantly engaged in wars and plundering at home and abroad.

During his reign, the schism between Sadducees and Pharisees reached the breaking point and civil war ensued. Although most of the Maccabees had originally been Pharisees, the current secular, financial, and imperial interests of their kingly successors had drawn them deeper and deeper into the Sadducee camp. But during this same time, the Pharisees were gaining ever-greater power and influence amongst the majority of the people. "It could only be with deep-seated resentment," writes Emil Schürer in *A History of the Jewish People in the Time of Jesus*, "that pious Jews could look on and see a wild warrior like Alexander Janneus discharging the duties of high priest in the holy place, certainly not with the conscientious and painstaking observance of the ordinances regarded by the Pharisees as divine. Even while he was discharging his priestly office it is said that for the first time they broke out in open rebellion."[4] Apparently, during the Feast of Tabernacles, Alexander was pelted by the assembled people with lemon-like fruits called citrons that were used as part of the ceremony. He responded by calling in his soldiers and massacring six hundred people.

This action soon led to a general rebellion, and Alexander spent six years fighting his own people and killing 50,000 of them. Then the Pharisees made a mistake. They asked the latest Seleucid Emperor, Demetrius, for help. Demetrius was only too happy to oblige. He arrived with his army, and Alexander was forced to flee into the mountains. But this renewed invasion by the Greek Seleucids was too much for many of the Pharisees: they realized too late that they would rather be ruled by a bad Jewish king than by this Hellenist foreigner. Six thousand of them went back to Alexander, and together they forced Demetrius to withdraw. Once he was out of danger, however, Alexander wrought a terrible vengeance on the Pharisees. According to Josephus Flavius, he crucified eight hundred of them, and while they were still alive they had to watch the slaughter of their wives and children. During that night of horror, eight thousand Pharisees fled from Judea, following which there was finally peace in the land for the remaining years of Alexander's rule.

When he died in 78 BCE, his will named his wife Alexandra, widowed yet again by a Hasmonean king, as successor to the throne. Alexandra turned out to be the direct opposite of her husband, and the most capable of all the Hasmonean rulers. She befriended the Pharisees, invited the banished to come home, and gave them most of the power in her government. Her piety and conscientiousness made her the Pharasaic standard of a God-fearing ruler. She instituted vast social reforms, including free elementary schools for girls and boys that virtually eliminated illiteracy. During her reign from 78 - 69 BCE, the nation prospered, and her era has been referred to as a brief Golden Age.

But this turned out to be just a brief respite, and complete chaos and final destruction followed almost immediately.

Alexandra had two sons. The eldest, Hyrcanus II, was a Pharisee. The other, Aristobulus II, was a Sadducee. Unable to assume the High Priesthood herself (only men were allowed), she named Hyrcanus II to the post. When she died, Hyrcanus grabbed the throne as well. But Aristobulus then led a revolt, and with the help of the priesthood he deposed Hyrcanus. As a result, another civil war between Pharisees and Sadducees broke out in 67 BCE.

Now it was Hyrcanus' turn once again. Under the guidance and encouragement of Antipater – the Governor of the neighboring Idumeans who had been forcefully converted to Judaism by John Hyrcanus – and with an army of neighboring Arabians led by the Arabian Prince Aretas, Hyrcanus was able to wrest the throne back again from his brother.

But Aristobulus refused to give up. He now appealed to the Romans for help. It happened that, right at this time, the

Roman general Pompey had just finished his conquest of the Seleucid Empire, and he and his army were right next door. Pompey listened to envoys (and received plenty of gifts) from both brothers. Then he told Hyrcanus' friend Aretas to withdraw his troops if he did not wish to be declared an enemy of Rome, and Aristobulus was returned to power a second time.

But it was still not over! In 63 BCE, Pompey was again in the neighborhood conquering more Greek lands for the Romans. This time, he was met by representatives of *three* Jewish parties. Hyrcanus pleaded to be reinstated. Aristobulus pleaded to keep his job. And the Pharisees, who had had enough of all such kings, pleaded with Pompey to recognize neither of them, and to return the country to the rule of a legitimate High Priest.

But this time, rather than siding with any of them, Pompey marched into Palestine and conquered it, and he renamed it Judea. Those who resisted were beheaded. Territories that had been conquered by the Hasmoneans were taken away and became part of the newly formed Roman province of Syria. A much reduced Judea was turned over to Hyrcanus, who was given the position of High Priest, but was no longer a king. Aristobulus was taken by Pompey back to Rome as a prisoner of war, where he was made to march in front of the conqueror's chariot.

After just seventy-six years, the great-grandchildren of the original Maccabees had lost that freedom which Mattathias' courage and Judah Maccabee's valor had won for them, and the second Kingdom of Judah had become a vassal state of the Roman Empire.

CHAPTER SEVEN

Rome

According to legend, around the time the Assyrians were preparing to conquer and disperse the northern ten tribes of Israel, a king named Numitor was usurped by his younger brother, Amulius, who took over the throne in the city of Alba Longa in Italy.

Numitor had a daughter, Rhea Silvia, and Amulius was afraid she might one day bear a son who would demand back the throne. So he had her sent to the temple of the goddess Vesta, and she became one of the Vestal Virgins who tended the temple. But despite these precautions, the god Mars ravished her, and she gave birth to twins whom she named Romulus and Remus.

When he heard that two heirs had been born, Amulius had Rhea Silvia buried alive and the twins were put in a basket and thrown into the Tiber River. But the Tiber overflowed its banks and so, rather than drowning, the twins were washed ashore.

A she-wolf came upon them, took pity on them, and nursed them alongside her own cubs. Soon they were found by a herdsman named Faustulus, who took them home and raised them as his own sons. They grew into brave young men who robbed bandits and returned the spoils to the shepherds.

One day, at a Feast, they chanced to meet the former king, Numitor, and while talking together it soon became clear that they were his grandsons. They decided to avenge their mother and grandfather – they killed Amulius and put Numitor back on the throne of Alba Longa.

Some time later, Alba Longa became too crowded for them, so they moved on and started a new settlement of their own on the shores of the Tiber. But both were ambitious, and they became jealous of each other. Eventually, an argument over the meaning of an omen turned into a fight. Romulus slew Remus, and named the settlement after himself – Rome.

However that may be, in about 509 BCE, shortly after the Persian King Cyrus had allowed the Jewish exiles to return home and rebuild their Temple, the Romans expelled the ruling Etruscans (a highly civilized race that had preceded them in Italy) and set up a Republic, with Senators elected from amongst the wealthy patrician families. The Senators would then select two Consuls, who served in place of the Etruscan king.

By 387 BCE, just prior to the time of Alexander the Great, the city of Rome began acquiring new land and started building an empire of its own. By 265 BCE, while Palestine was in the hands of the Ptolemies, the Romans had conquered and unified most of the Italian peninsula.

They then went to war against Carthage (also called Puncia), a great city on the northern coast of Africa. Carthage controlled the rich island of Sicily which was just off the coast of Italy, and Rome soon took it from them. There were altogether three wars with Carthage, known as the Punic Wars. In the second one, a generation after the first, Rome was nearly captured by the Carthaginian general Hannibal, who fooled the Romans and attacked by land rather than by sea: he led his army over the Alps on elephants. But he was forced to return to his homeland and defend it against Roman soldiers in 202 BCE, and there the Romans defeated him. Later, in the third Punic War in 146 BCE, while Judah Maccabee was defeating the Seleucids, Rome attacked Carthage a third time and completely destroyed the city, slaughtering most of the citizens and selling the rest into slavery.

By the end of the second Punic War, Rome was already a rich and powerful empire. But the Republic had been set up as a form of government designed to rule a city, not an empire, and as time went on the Senate was not up to the job. The Republic's days were numbered.

In 60 BCE, Pompey (who we have already met while he was conquering the Greeks) and Crassus were the two Consuls. Another ambitious general, Julius Caesar, convinced the Senate to name him as a third Consul. The trio became known as the First Triumvirate. The following year, Caesar was made governor of the northwest territory of Gaul (roughly modern France), and from there he led an army which soon conquered most of western Europe. These exploits made him extremely popular in his home city.

In 49 BCE, a jealous Senate ordered him home – but they told him to leave his army behind. Smelling trouble, he came as ordered but he brought the entire army with him. The Senate then told Pompey to attack, but Caesar's army routed him and Pompey and his army fled to Greece. Caesar pursued him, conquered his army, and Pompey then fled to Egypt. When Caesar reached Egypt, in 47 BCE, the ten-year-old vassal king, Ptolemy XIII, presented Pompey's severed head to Caesar.

The young Ptolemy governed Egypt in conjunction with his older sister, Cleopatra – who was a Grecian princess of the Ptolemaic family, not (as is often assumed) an Egyptian. Caesar fell in love with her, he helped her get rid of her younger brother, and she gave birth to his son.

Caesar then returned to Rome and the people proclaimed him 'Dictator for Life'. Many Senators, however, were outraged by this turn of events, and on March 15, in 44 BCE, a mob of sixty Senators, including Brutus and Cassius, attacked him and murdered him.

At first, an amnesty was declared. But at Caesar's funeral, his friend and military colleague, Marc Antony, read aloud Caesar's Will – which left most of his property to the Roman people – and he then roused the populace against the conspirators who were forced to flee for their lives.

The Senate then appointed Caesar's generals, Marc Antony and Lepidus, and his nephew Octavian, to lead the Republic as the Second Triumvirate. Lepidus soon retired (apparently under duress from Octavian), and before long Antony and Octavian squared off for total control of the empire.

Antony led an army to Egypt, where he, too, fell in love with Cleopatra (despite being married to Octavian's sister). They conspired to oust Octavian and rule the Roman Empire together, but the people distrusted this foreign princess – especially after Octavian discovered and leaked Antony's Will, which left his money to Cleopatra – and they favored Octavian. In 31 BCE, in the Battle of Actium on the Mediterranean Sea, Octavian defeated the forces of Antony and Cleopatra. The lovers soon committed suicide, and Octavian became the sole ruler of Rome.

He never called himself "emperor", but the Senate knew that the army was completely loyal to him and he could do as he pleased. The people gave him the title 'Augustus' (*the Respected One*), they began to worship him as a god, and he ruled for 41 years, from 27 B.C.E until his death in 14 AD. Toward the end of his life he could truthfully say, "I left Rome a city of marble, though I found it a city of bricks."

Roman Palestine

After the conquest of Palestine by Pompey, there had been a period of relative peace. But soon Aristobulus escaped from Rome, returned home, and began vying against his brother Hyrcanus once again, trying to regain control of the government. He was soon captured and sent a second time to Rome. But in 49 BCE, when Pompey fled Italy and Caesar established himself in Rome, Caesar wished to make use of Aristobulus – so he was released from prison, given two legions, and told to go to Syria and fight Pompey. But Pompey's friends got hold of him first and poisoned him. His son, Alexander, was also captured by a relative of Pompey, and was beheaded.

After the defeat of Pompey and his death in 48 BCE, Hyrcanus' old friend Antipater (the clever Idumean who was *really* in charge of Palestine) immediately attached himself to the party of Caesar: he knew that his safety and his power now depended on Caesar's good graces. So when Caesar went to Egypt and was fighting (along with Cleopatra) against the forces of young Ptolemy XIII, Antipater had Hyrcanus send three thousand troops to aid Caesar. He also saw to it that all the Jews who were then living in Egypt sided with Caesar. Afterwards, in the summer of 47 BCE, Caesar rewarded them by coming through Syria and meeting with them both, showing them much favor. Hyrcanus, whose power had been limited to the High Priesthood, was given back his political authority and named a 'friend' of Rome. But Antipater was named *Procurator* of Judea – a confirmation of the higher authority he already had. Many territorial possessions that had been taken from Judea by Pompey were now returned.

Caesar's policy was to keep the provinces contented, so Palestine had several years of peace and prosperity, and the Jews in Judea and throughout the empire were free to exercise their religion undisturbed. When Caesar was murdered a few years later, no foreign people were more sorrowful than the people of Judea.

After the assassination, Brutus fled to Macedonia and Cassius fled to Syria. Cassius soon established himself as the master of Syria, and to maintain his army he needed money. Antipater, ever the opportunist, now allied himself with Cassius, and he and his son Herod raised tax money in Judea for Cassius' army.

The following year, Antipater was poisoned by a relative. After his death, Herod avenged his father's death by having the murderer assassinated by hired thugs who were supplied by Cassius. Cassius, meanwhile, bled the region dry with his demand for taxes, and when they could not be paid he sold Jewish citizens into slavery to raise the needed funds.

Then, in 42 BCE, Cassius and Brutus were defeated in battle by Antony and Octavian, and the administration of Palestine fell to the lot of Antony. Early the next year Jewish representatives met with Antony, asked that their countrymen who had been sold by Cassius into slavery be freed, and made complaints about Herod. The first request was granted. But many years earlier, while serving under Caesar in the region, Antony had been an intimate friend of Antipater. He now extended this friendship to Antipater's son, Herod. Hyrcanus was once again stripped of political authority, and Herod was named Governor of Judea. Antony himself now embarked on a life of luxury, and like Cassius before him he needed money. Herod helped supply it.

In 40 BCE, Antony spent part of the year in Egypt under the enchantment of Cleopatra, and the rest of the year in Italy attending to various affairs. In his absence, the Parthians, a people from Iran who were related to the Persians and who had long been a thorn in the side of Rome, invaded Antony's Asian territories and took over control of much of it, including Syria. A surviving son of Aristobulus, named Antigonus, persuaded them to help him secure the Jewish throne. They captured Hyrcanus, cut off his ears (a mutilation that, according to Mosaic Law, made him thereafter ineligible to serve as High Priest), and they chased away Herod. They put Antigonus on the throne. Then they plundered the land, before taking Hyrcanus as a prisoner and going home.

Antigonus then declared himself both King and High Priest of Judea. Herod, in the meantime, sailed to Rome and went to see his friend Antony. Afterwards, he met with Octavian as well, and he secured the goodwill of them both – probably with a mixture of clever rhetoric and expensive bribery. As a result, he was taken before the Roman Senate, and they formally named him King of Judea.

Taking possession of the throne, however, would now prove difficult, for the Parthians and their puppet Antigonus were in control of the country. Herod returned to the region, raised an army with Antony's help, and began a long battle with the Parthians. Finally, in 37 BCE, he laid siege upon the capital city of Jerusalem and eventually stormed it and overran it. Antigonus was chained and led away to his death. And so it was that the Idumean Herod, three years after his appointment by the Romans, effectively became the King of the Jews.

Herod "the Great"

It was not an easy job. The people of Judea, who were almost completely in the hands of the Pharisees, were loathe to accept the domination of this Idumean half-Jew who was on such close terms with the Romans. He also had enemies among the friends of Antigonus, though he quickly executed many of them and confiscated their property. And there was still the royal Hasmonean family to consider, though he had recently joined himself to them in marriage: during the siege of Jerusalem, Herod had married Miriam, the granddaughter of Hyrcanus. His new mother-in-law, Alexandra, hated him with a passion, and was always a threat. On the other hand, Hyrcanus himself had been released by the Parthians and had come home, and Herod, who had always been on good terms with the old man, continued this friendship.

Since Hyrcanus could no longer serve as High Priest, Herod had to appoint a new one. Alexandra demanded that her son, Miriam's brother Aristobulus (another one of the same name), be chosen. Miriam of course agreed, and Alexandra even managed to persuade Cleopatra to convince Antony to order Herod to appoint her son. Herod did so, but he could not rid himself of his distrust for the Hasmoneans (despite a great love for Miriam), and he soon arranged to have Aristobulus 'accidentally' killed in 35 BCE. Although Alexandra managed to get Antony to summon Herod in order that he might answer for the crime, Herod was pronounced innocent by his friend and he returned to Jerusalem.

While he was with Antony, he had left his wife under the protection of his sister's husband Joseph, ordering him to kill Miriam if he, Herod, did not return – rather than allowing any other man to ever obtain his beloved. Later, when he was safely home, his sister Salome accused her own husband of having had illicit sex with Miriam, and Joseph was promptly executed.

Not long after this, in 32 BCE, the war broke out between Antony and Octavian which ended two years later with Antony's defeat and suicide. Herod quickly took steps to endear himself to the winner: when soldiers of Antony tried to leave Egypt to engage Octavian in further battle, Herod stopped them. He then went off to present himself to the new Caesar. Before he left, however, just to make sure there were no Hasmonean coups during his absence, he had his poor aged friend Hyrcanus executed on fake charges of conspiracy.

He was then so skillful in the meeting with his new friend Octavian that his royal rank was confirmed and even more territories were added to his kingdom.

While he was away this time, Herod had once again left orders that, if he failed to return, Miriam should be killed. And again he came home only to hear rumors of illicit sex with her guardian. This time, Herod had them *both* executed. Afterwards, though, he repented his murder, mourned his beloved wife excessively, and nearly killed himself with remorse and bouts of drinking. During this time, his mother-in-law Alexandra began scheming against him once again. But Herod recovered from his melancholy just in time, discovered her plans, and she too was executed in 28 BCE.

Following this murder spree, things settled down a bit and Herod entered into his period of glory, for which he sometimes receives the appellation 'Herod the Great' (not, however, from the Jewish community, who always remember him as a corrupt and vicious murderer). During the years from 25 BCE to 13 BCE, he built extravagant temples and theaters and palaces, whole new cities were constructed in lavish style (several of them named in honor of himself), parks and gardens were created, and he surrounded himself with emblems of Greek philosophy, literature, and art.

Herod had no real interest in Judaism – according to Flavius Josephus, he boasted that he was more nearly related to the Greeks than to the Jews. But the Pharisees were now such a powerful force in Judean society that he could not afford to offend them with too much Hellenization. So his paramount achievement during these years was his restoration of the Jewish Temple (of course, he also built lots of pagan temples). When Herod came to power, the Second Temple, despite frequent renovations, was small and rundown. When Herod was finished it was the height of splendor, gleaming with white marble and gold. According to Josephus:

> [The doors of the Temple] were adorned with embroidered veils, with their flowers of purple, and pillars interwoven; and over these, but under the crown-work, was spread out a golden vine, with its branches hanging down from a great height, the largeness and fine workmanship of which was a surprising sight to the spectators, to see what vast materials there were, and with what great skill the workmanship was done. He also encompassed the entire temple with very large cloisters, contriving them to be in a due proportion thereto; and he laid out larger sums of money upon them than had been done before him, till it seemed that no one else had so greatly adorned the temple as he had done. There was a large wall to both the cloisters, which wall was itself the most prodigious work that was ever heard of by man.[5]

Herod appeased the Pharisees by making sure that everything was accomplished according to their convictions – only priests were allowed to build the inner sanctuary, there were no statues or graven images, etc. But despite its material magnificence the Temple was spiritually rather empty: there was still no Ark. And as a final touch, as if out of spite, Herod had a great Roman Eagle erected over the entrance.

Although this period of Herod's reign was glorious in many ways, the people were far from content. He kept his citizenry in line by means of taxes, violence, and murder. He was ever-vigilant, punishing any suspicion of rebellion. According to Schürer, "All idle loitering about the streets, all common assemblies, yea, even meeting together on the street, was forbidden. And when anything of the kind was nevertheless done, the king had information about it immediately conveyed to him by his secret spies."[6]

> Only by force could the people be brought to
> tolerate the semi-pagan rule of the Idumean;
> and only his despotic, iron hand prevented
> an uprising of the fermenting masses.[7]

The final period of Herod's rule, from 13 BCE until his death in 4 BCE, were years of family turmoil.

Herod had several sons. The eldest, named Antipater after Herod's father, was the son of his first wife, Doris. He had long ago banished them both, and Antipater was only allowed in Jerusalem during certain holidays. Miriam had given him five sons and a daughter: the two oldest, and historically the most important, were called Alexander and Aristobulus. A third wife had given him a son he named after himself, Herod Antipas. There were several other wives and other children as well, including Archelaus and Philip.

After he murdered Miriam, Herod had sent her sons, Alexander and Aristobulus, to Rome to be educated. Five years later, he fetched them home again. As Miriam's children, the boys were Hasmoneans. At first, this did not seem to be a problem for their father. But over time, and with the help of slanderous rumors from Herod's sister Salome, he began to look upon them with suspicion.

In a misguided effort to balance out a danger that only he was imagining, he brought back his first son, Antipater. It was a bad move. Antipater used the opportunity to incessantly slander Herod, and to turn his younger brothers against their father. Soon the boys were complaining openly about the death of their mother, as well as the treatment they themselves were being accorded by their suspicious father. The family rift kept widening, and eventually, in 12 BCE, Herod went to Augustus and accused his two sons of treason. Augustus, finding the whole thing a bit silly, succeeded in reconciling them and he sent them home. But the reconciliation did not last. Before long, the sons of Miriam were imprisoned, and sometime around 7 BCE Herod had them executed. Antipater, who, unbeknownst to Herod, had instigated the boys, was now his father's favorite. But within a few years he was found out, and Herod had him executed just five days before his own death in 4 BCE.

According to the *Gospel of Matthew*, it was also during these final bloody months of Herod's life that he heard rumors of the birth of a Jewish Savior who might one day rival his throne, and he imitated Pharaoh (in the story of Moses) and Nimrod (in the story of Abraham) by ordering the execution of all young children in Bethlehem.

In the days before his death Herod kept writing new Wills, naming various remaining sons as his successor. After he was gone, the sons fought with each other and carved up the kingdom – with Augustus' help – into three separate pieces, ruled respectively by Herod Antipas (in Perea and Galilee), Philip (in the region east and northeast of the Sea of Galilee), and Archelaus (in Judea, including Jerusalem, as well as Samaria and Idumea).

Philip, the exception in his family, appears to have been a man of moderation who governed well.

Herod Antipas, on the other hand, was much like his father – ambitious, sly, and ruthless – though not as competent. John the Baptist and Jesus would both soon make their appearance in his realm, John in Perea and Jesus in Galilee.

Archelaus proved to be a hateful tyrant. He was immediately confronted with rebelliousness, which he crushed violently. He appointed and removed High Priests illegally. He entered into a religiously forbidden marriage. Finally, after nine years, overwhelming complaints to Rome persuaded Augustus to remove him and place the region under the jurisdiction of a Roman Procurator (the Procurator from 26 CE to 36 CE would be Pontius Pilate).

This greatly changed the social complexion of Judea. Despite their friendship with Rome, Herod and his sons understood and usually respected the Jewish traditions, and had been careful not to offend the Pharisees with excessive Hellenization. The Romans, however, had no appreciation for such niceties. They could never understand, in Schurer's words, "how a whole people would offer the most persistent resistance unto death, and would suffer annihilation on account of merely ceremonial rites and what seemed matters of indifference."[8] The Jews, on the other hand, perceived every Roman command, no matter how simple, as an encroachment on their sacred rights and their duties to God. Coupled with the insolence and corruption of the petty rulers sent by Rome, the inevitable result was ever-increasing hostility and fanaticism.

CHAPTER EIGHT

Palestine in the Time of Jesus

The religion of the old Persian Empire was *Zoroastrism*. According to Zoroaster, the universe was created by the one great god, *Ahura Mazda*. The created world was 'Good', and was governed by a cosmological force called *asha*, which literally means 'Truth' – more accurately, *asha* was an ordering and harmonizing force substantially analogous to the later Greek concept of *the Logos*.

As a result of the Free Will which existed in Ahura Mazda's universe, *violations* of this order were possible and did arise. These violations represented a new, universal, negative force called *druj* – which literally means 'the Lie', and is a concept similar to the Greek *Chaos*. The purpose of mankind, according to Zoroaster, was to assist in the maintaining of the cosmological order. But Ahura Mazda gave humanity Free Will so that they could choose to do 'good' on behalf of *asha*, or 'evil' on behalf of *druj*.

During their long contact with the Persian Empire, the Jews had absorbed this idea of life as a battle between Good and Evil. Now, in Judea, the line between Good and Evil seemed to have been clearly drawn between the Jews and the Romans.

This divisiveness was further fueled by many things that had been brewing for a very long time:

First, there was the growing anger and cynicism caused by the corruption and violence of their own kings and the High Priesthood. Various new groups and 'movements' – particularly the Pharisees, Sadducees, Zealots, and Essenes – were shaped and motivated by these sentiments.

The Sadducees, as we have seen, were mostly members of the wealthy conservative elite. They had opened their hearts to the secular world of Greek culture and commerce, while insisting that the only worthy form of Judaism was to be found in a rather spiritless, fundamentalist, "pure letter-of-the-law" reading of the Torah. Philosophically, they denied such concepts as resurrection, personal immortality, or other ideas that were only found in the *oral* tradition. Politically, they contented themselves with the way things were and resisted change, preferring instead to promote cordial relations with the Romans. Although they often held influential positions in society, they were unpopular with the masses who generally opposed all foreign influences.

The Pharisees, the largest group, were mostly middle-class Jews who emphasized the exact keeping of the law as it had been interpreted by sages, elders, and rabbis. Politically, they were ardent anti-Hellenists and anti-Romans. The Pharisees were admired by the majority of Jews, but they were never a very large group since most people had neither the education nor the time to join the party and follow all their stringent rules regarding prayer, fasting, festival observance, tithing, etc. Pharisees were greatly influenced by Persian ideas of Good and Evil, and they adhered to the growing belief in the resurrection of the body with an afterlife of rewards and punishments. Over time, many of the finer impulses of Pharisaism would weaken into an empty religious formalism (as is ever the case), focusing on outward actions rather than the inward experience of the soul. Although the group had initially been exceedingly tolerant, this began to deteriorate into a feeling of contempt toward those Jews who did not meet their standards of behavior.

From among the more politically radical of the Pharisees there came a new group called the *Zealots*, meaning 'men of action'. These were revolutionary patriots, who sought to overthrow the Roman regime by whatever means necessary. They were strongest in Galilee. As the Romans committed one atrocity after another, the ranks of the Zealots grew. (By 66 CE their ranks would be swollen, and they would lead the charge against the Roman oppressors, initiating a long, costly, and bitter war, that finally ended with the inevitable Roman victory and the destruction of the Second Temple in 70 CE).

At the other extreme were the Essenes. These were religious Jews who, in contrast with the Sadducees, now *rejected* the Temple and the Priesthood believing that these had been defiled by corruption and murder. They also scorned what they felt was the spiritually empty and overly 'comfortable' life of the Pharisees. And unlike the Zealots, they had no taste for politics or violence. They chose, instead, to withdraw from secular activities and devote themselves entirely to spiritual purification and contemplation within austere religious communities. The Essenes are not mentioned in the New Testament, but Flavius Josephus, Philo, Pliny, and various others speak of them in their writings. According to the evidence of the Dead Sea Scrolls that were discovered in 1947, and the additional scrolls that were later excavated from a Jewish monastery in Qumran, the Essene communities worked and worshipped according to their own customs, studied and copied religious literature, practiced baptism[*] and a communion meal, and lived an ascetic life devoted to spiritual growth and the perfection of the soul.

Another source of seething hostility in Palestine was a peculiar new experience of the times, the phenomenon called 'religious persecution'. People had often wondered why God allowed good people to suffer *despite* their being good. But now, as the Jews found themselves being

---

[*] The Essenes practiced an initiatory purification ritual that included immersion in a ritual pool called a *mikvah* (*mikvahs* still exist). John the Baptist and his followers were most probably members of an Essene community, and so, some suspect, was Jesus.

persecuted simply because of their religious practices, they began to wonder why it was that God would allow people to suffer *because* they were good! Such persecution seemed the very essence of Evil.

Fortunately, the belief in a cosmic struggle between Good and Evil carried with it a growing conviction that Good would ultimately triumph. Therefore, the experience of religious persecution, according to Julie Galambush in *The Reluctant Parting*, "proved to be the catalyst for a developing belief that those who died for their faith in this world would be rewarded in *another* world – life after death through resurrection."[9] Rather than being seen as unfortunate *wretches* who had been unaccountably forgotten by God, such people began to be seen as *martyrs* – religious heroes whom God would reward in the afterlife for their goodness and their faithfulness.

The philosophical belief that God – and Good – would ultimately triumph over Evil, coupled with rising political tension with Rome and the anticipation of inevitable war, led to an increasingly 'apocalyptic' view of the world: in other words, many Jews in Palestine began to believe that the end of the world (at least as we know it) was rapidly approaching – in a physical, external sense. God was about to triumph over Evil, He would judge the wicked, He would reward the just, and a New Order would dawn.

To lead God's legions to victory against hopelessly adverse political conditions, and to establish a new kingdom of God, a leader with divine power would be necessary. And thus, a messianic hope was kindled in the heart of Judaism. God had promised Samuel that an anointed son of David would rule over the Israelites forever. Where was he? Now, after centuries of Assyrian, Babylonian, Persian, Greek, and Roman oppression, faith in God and hope for the future combined into the belief that God was finally going to send *Moshiach,* "the anointed one", the *Messiah*, to rescue Israel and lead them to a new world. As Galambush writes:

> Messianic expectations, cosmic dualism, martyrdom, and resurrection – an entire constellation of beliefs absent from ancient Israelite religion – suddenly took center stage. In some respects Jewish life continued as it had done for centuries: the rituals in the Jerusalem temple followed forms set down in Leviticus, and the rhythm of Sabbath and the festivals went on as always. But in the final centuries before the Common Era, Jewish popular imagination had come to occupy a far more colorful religious landscape, one in which history was fast approaching its end.[10]

It was into this colorful, dangerous, and hopeful world that a child called Jesus, of the Tribe of Judah and the House of David, was born in Bethlehem.

INDEX

NOTES

1   Hooker, Richard, *Ancient Greece, The Athenian Empire,* http://www.wsu.edu:8080/~dee/GREECE/ATHEMP.HTM, 1996

2   Plato, *Republic, Book VI, s. 510, (Jowett), p. 250*

3   ibid p. 251

4   Schurer, Emil, *A History of the Jewish People in the Time of Jesus*, Schocken Books, 1961, p. 178

5   Flavius Josephus, *Antiquities of the Jews* (ed. William Whiston), Book 15, ch 11, http://www.perseus.tufts.edu/cgi-bin/ptext?doc= Perseus%Atext%3A1999.01.0146

6   Schurer, ibid p. 146

7   ibid p. 151

8   ibid p. 178

9   Galambush, Julie, *The Reluctant Parting*, HarperColins, NY, 2005, p. 7

10   ibid p. 8

2649668